5/74

2.00

SOFTWARE SELECTION

Susan Wooldridge

FIRST EDITION

petrocelli books. New York 1973

Copyright © Mason & Lipscomb Publishers, Inc., 1973

Published simultaneously in the United Kingdom by Mason & Lipscomb Publishers, Inc., London, England.

Second Printing, December, 1973.

Printed in the United States of America.

Library of Congress Cataloging in Publication Data

Library of Congress Cataloging in Publication Data

Wooldridge, Susan, 1940-
    Software selection.

    Bibliography: p.
    1. Electronic data processing departments--
Management. 2. Computer programs. I. Title.
HF5548.2.W66   658'.05'425   73-7523
ISBN 0-88405-034-3
Formerly 0-87769-157-6

For my father

Other books by the same author

Computer Survival Handbook, with Keith R. London
Security Standards for Data Processing, with Colin R. Corder and
   Claude R. Johnson

CONTENTS

PREFACE

This book is written for those in data processing who have the task of choosing software for their computer installations. There are more than 600 organizations in the United States offering software for sale, and at least as many again in the United Kingdom and Europe. As computer manufacturers increasingly adopt the policy of unbundling programming services, users are faced with the problems of choosing from available software packages or of compiling their own programs.

The data processing manager has at his disposal three tangible resources: people, money, and machines. The power and variety of computers is steadily increasing while the cost per amount of processing, however measured, is decreasing. Further, over the long term, the supply of money tends to increase (at least in successful companies) as the economy expands and business becomes more and more dependent on computers to support its activities. The supply of data processing people, however (programmers, systems analysts, and managers), seems to be continually decreasing while salaries are continually increasing. This situation is not one of sudden emergence, nor has it been caused by unidentifiable influences. The picture is one of rows and rows of computers coming off the assembly line, each demanding to be fed with programs. Data processing departments the world over labor night and day to create the programs to feed them, but still cannot cope with the increasing volume and are gradually getting further and further behind in their efforts to satisfy these insatiable demands.

It is known that one solution to the panic is to use programs already written by systems houses—that is, systems software and applications packages. What is surprising is that this is not done more often. Why, for example, as has happened recently in Britain, would as many as 200 different companies employ programmers to write an equal number of sales analysis packages, without one of them considering the use of programs written by a systems house? Or even a prewritten program for *part* of the job? Perhaps the best answers to these questions have been turned up by surveys, which showed that the most common reason for not using packaged programs is unawareness that they exist.

To make economic use of computers, managers *must* become more diligent in seeking out all possible solutions to a data processing problem, and they must become more knowledgeable in choosing the one best adapted to their particular situation. This book is aimed at helping with those tasks. It gives practical advice on finding and evaluating packages, without losing sight of the fact that a package is only one of several possible solutions to any particular problem. Because unbundling means that "free" compilers and operating systems will soon be history, this text covers both systems software and applications packages. It is written for managers, analysts, systems programmers, and all others who are concerned with finding, judging, and using software in commercial installations.

This writer assumes that the reader is familiar with the components of computer hardware and with the way in which data processing departments are organized and operate. Of necessity, there is some discussion of the way in which in-house systems are developed and of problems that exist regardless of whether purchased software is a consideration. For the most part, however, little is said about general material on documentation, file conversion, system implementation methods, and the like, which are not peculiar to the selection and use of software and which have been more than adequately covered in other books.

I would like to thank the many companies and individuals who have taken an interest in this book and have supplied material and suggestions for inclusion in it. Especially are thanks due my husband for his cooperation and patience in maintaining domestic equilibrium during my compilation of the manuscript.

Susan Wooldridge

PART ONE

SOFTWARE IN THE COMMERCIAL ENVIRONMENT

1 | THE NATURE OF SOFTWARE?

The compilers of data processing dictionaries and glossaries have an almost hopeless task of standardizing terminology and nomenclature in the computer world. The industry is characterized by the truly amazing quantity of jargon it has generated in its brief history. True, every business has its particular set of specialized terms, all of which have evolved from a like situation. Insurance companies are a good example, but their "language" has had about three hundred years in which to stabilize, whereas the brief history of the computer has spawned an endless array of terms that duplicate, conflict, and confuse each other. The situation is complicated by the fact that new terms are invented daily and old ones are modified through usage or come to have altogether different meanings. Also, some words used to describe the same specialized technique or concept may mean different things to different people. Computer manufacturers are particularly apt to invent a new word for something that has been around a long time and already has a perfectly good name—or several. For example, the two top "zone punches" on cards have been called R and X, X and Y, 10 and 11, and 11 and 12 at various times by various companies. At the time this book is being written, one organization is attempting to classify and define only those data processing terms that apply to software and the application of software. It has collected over 3000 different terms and is still working on it.

DEFINING SOFTWARE

No commonly recognized set of definitions is available. Even the U.S. Internal Revenue Service has had difficulty in defining terms, and one for which they have been unable to find a single satisfactory definition is *software*.

It is not the purpose of this book to try to establish or promulgate standard definitions of software terms. Organizations and individuals who have tried this in the past have usually ended up by creating yet another set of definitions for the same old words plus a few new ones, making the situation even worse. Instead, an attempt will be made to put into words what most people in data processing intuitively understand to be the meanings of the most commonly used words and phrases having to do with software, and to point out overlapping and duplicate meanings. Along with this, the categories into which various types of software fall will be described. Finally, the terms chosen for use for the rest of this book will be stated.

First of all, consider the word "software" itself, which has several levels of meaning. In its broadest sense, it encompasses everything that is not hardware: programs, languages, manuals, documentation, and in some contexts even the process of writing programs. In a somewhat more restrictive sense, it refers to instructions for the computer which are resident in memory at the time they are being executed. This covers all types of programs. In its most narrow sense, problem programs (those designed for processing a particular set of files to produce a prespecified output) are excluded, leaving most manufacturer-supplied programs plus "utilities" written in house and those acquired from other sources. Expressed rigorously, this definition is:

Software: A routine, program, or set of programs that is generalized to perform the same processing function(s) for a number of users.

Processing functions include such things as sorting, merging, data transfers (from memory to a file, or vice versa), file and record handling, and the preparation of reports, if this is done under control of parameter specifications and is unrelated to the content of the report being formatted and produced. A single program may perform only one of these functions (e.g., a sort) or may perform several of them.

The definition given above will be assumed in this book by the word "software" when it is used in a general sense without any qualifications. It therefore excludes programs written by a single user for use only on his machine for processing a particular set of files. However, if a user writes such a system, runs it in his own installation, and then decides it meets a general processing problem, he may sell or give it to another company for its use. In this case, the program then comes under this definition of software because it is to a certain extent "generalized."

SOFTWARE CATEGORIES

Software as defined above is usually divided into two major groups: application independent, and application oriented.

Application-Independent Software

This type of software is a program or set of programs designed for use *without regard for the business environment in which it operates.* Such software is sometimes subdivided further into machine-oriented programs such as assemblers, compilers, and operating systems, and problem-oriented programs such as sorts and utilities. This distinction is rather a fine one, however, because a sort is much less oriented toward the solution of a particular problem than it is to a general class of problems such as getting a set of records, any set of records, into a predetermined sequence. In that this type of software is considered by the user to be so indispensable as to be almost an extension of the hardware, it is relatively more machine oriented than problem oriented.

Another term frequently used for application-independent software is *systems software*, which will be used in this book. Because these programs are designed around the internal environment of the computer, to directly or indirectly support problem-program processing, they are sometimes called "hard software," a term that in itself can have various shades of meaning. "Systems software" is preferred because it is more descriptive and is in more common usage.

Other classification methods are also popular, however. A few familiar ones include:

Operating support programs, which perform as extensions of the hardware system, and are resident in memory while problem programs are being executed, to control their operation. Examples are operating systems and system supervisors.

Programmer support programs, which assist in or take over completely the tasks that would otherwise fall to the programmer (e.g., MACROS: prewritten sets of instructions that the programmer can cause to be included automatically in his program by calling them in with special names. A large group of these handle input and output functions such as instructions to open, close, read, and write files). Other programmer support programs are compilers, assemblers, utility programs, and pre-processors of various types.

Data support programs, which perform file and record handling processes (sorts and merges), formatting and output production processes
(report generators), or a variety of functions (generalized file processors, to be discussed in more detail later).

Another category of software usually included in the term "application independent" is *programmer aids.* These are becoming increasingly popular.
They include debugging aids, coding shorthand pre-processors, flowcharting
programs and other documentation aids, test data generators, and job-control
language generators. It could be argued that these are application oriented because the application area is programming. However, since they are not an
end product in themselves but are used in the production of problem programs
of all types, and can be used in many different installations without regard for
the business environment, they will be included here under the heading of systems software.

Application-Oriented Software

Application-oriented software is defined as programs or systems designed to
perform automated data processing tasks for a specified area or areas of business but which may be used in more than one installation. These programs are
usually called "packages" because they may include a number of programs
along with operating instructions, documentation, and so on. Common examples of applications they serve are payroll, share registration, accounting
and costing, mass mailing, inventory management, cash-flow analysis, vehicle
scheduling, and production control. In fact, there is probably at least one
package available for every existing area of business. Most application-oriented
systems have certain characteristics in common:

1. They are intended for use "as is" or with slight modification.
2. They accept input in parameter form.
3. Output formats are usually fixed, but options may give some degree of
flexibility for report sequencing, data printing, and control breaks.

The general applicability, flexibility, and availability of this type of software varies tremendously and may range from small user-written systems
sold or given as an afterthought to another company, to large and extremely
sophisticated systems written by professionals in the software business,
heavily marketed, and expensive.

The term "package" or "applications package" will be used in this book for
this type of software. What may be included in the package will be discussed
in greater detail in a later chapter.

The advantages, disadvantages, and problems associated with the use of various types of software will be discussed in Chapter 3.

Specialized Applications

Other types of software fall into a gray area between those clearly designed for a particular application and those clearly independent. Examples are automated techniques, data processing department support programs, and generalized file processors.

Automated techniques such as PERT network and critical path analysis programs may be thought of as types of generalized application packages, for while they are designed to support the computer user rather than internal data processing or machine functions, they serve a wide variety of applications, from guided missile design to housing construction to book publishing. They are also sometimes used for control of systems and programming activities in large installations. It is not within the scope of this book to teach the use of such techniques.

Another automated technique finding more and more favor is decision table processing. Of course decision tables may be used within or outside the data processing department as a purely manual aid to documenting complex logical procedures, but when they are used by systems analysts and programmers as a more compact and more accurate substitute for flowcharts, it is usually worthwhile to extend their use a little more. Instead of coding from a decision table, the table itself can be computer-processed to produce either source or machine language statements automatically.

There are two types of decision table processor. The first is a pre-processor, which is a stand-alone program taking as input the decision table content and giving as output the source language statements to be included by the programmer in the main line of his program. Or, if the decision table covers all processing requirements, including input and output, the source statements produced may in themselves constitute a program. The other type of processor is a *macro*. The programmer writes the decision table statements as the operand of the macro. At compile time these produce machine language instructions in the main line of the program. There is at least one decision table processor for every major machine and language, and more are being developed all the time. The book on decision tables by K. R. London (40) not only describes the principles and usage of the technique generally, but also includes an excellent section on the automated processing of them.

Data processing department support programs include such things as project control and machine statistics packages, designed specifically for use within the data processing department for control and record keeping of its activities.

Strictly speaking, these are applications packages designed for a computer user
—the data processing department. On the other hand, they contribute indirectly toward efficient development and processing of other users' systems,
and are therefore classed in some installations as "systems software," at least
for budgeting purposes.

Generalized File Processor

In this survey of types of software available to today's computer user, close
attention must be paid to the type of package called a *generalized file processor*. Briefly defined, this is a system designed to handle file creation, file
maintenance, retrieval of individual data items on demand, and report generation, without regard for the application area in which it is used. To be a
truly generalized file processor, as the term is used in this book, the system
must at a minimum perform the four functions of file creation, maintenance,
retrieval, and reporting. Some of the processors available go far beyond this
and include such advanced facilities as decision table translation, automatic
internal sorting, flexible file structures that are automatically altered on the
basis of accumulated statistics on the retrieval requirements for the files, and
a wide variety of processing and output options. Some operate only in a batch
mode; others are real-time systems. Input and output routines are usually
modularized so that they can be changed easily, and some provide for user-
written routines to be inserted as required. Some are written for only one
type of machine; others are available for a variety of machines and configurations. Informatics' Mark IV is the most popular and probably the best known
of the generalized file processors.

This book will use the term "generalized file processor" for this type of
package. However, it is also known by many different names, including data
base management system, information management system, generalized program package, integrated data management system, generalized information
system, and all the various permutations and combinations of these words.

The earliest applications packages were, strictly speaking, designed for a
specific job, but included a variety of options so that they could be modified for other applications. Some of the smaller systems, although carrying
the name "generalized file processor," were no more than glorified report
generators. Today's larger, more popular systems are almost always the product of a manufacturer or professional software house that has set out to
write a system especially for a wide variety of requirements. Their prices
range widely, from a few thousand dollars to almost half a million when extra
options, implementation support, and modifications are added in.

Relationship of Different Types

The Venn diagram in Figure 1 illustrates the relationships of the various types of software discussed here. The degree of overlap between them is shown. For example, applications packages are shown within problem programs because they are a type of system for handling processing that would otherwise be done by handwritten programs. Decision table processors are both an extension of systems software and an aid to the programmer because they reduce the amount of hand coding required.

FIGURE 1: TYPES OF SOFTWARE

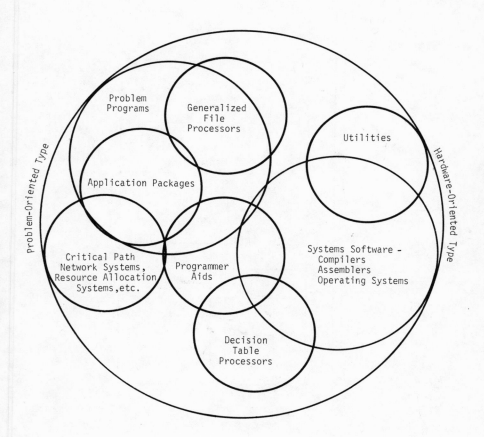

Figure 2 illustrates the relative degree of generalization of software, ranging from tailored problem programs at the top to very generalized systems software at the bottom. There is some degree of overlap here as well; for example, advanced generalized file processor may be on a par with systems software, but a very simple one may be best suited for particular applications areas and be no more generalized than an applications package.

FIGURE 2: RELATIVE DEGREE OF GENERALIZATION
OF VARIOUS TYPES OF SOFTWARE

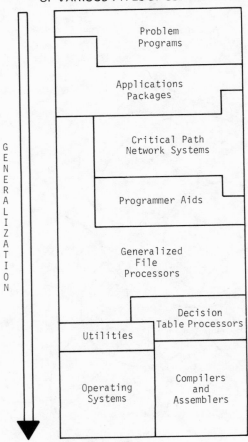

SOFTWARE SUPPLIERS

A number of organizations develop and supply software for today's market. First, of course, are the computer manufacturers. Through the first and second generations, and well into the third, much of what they supplied was "free." These gratuitous elements included all basic systems software, utilities, and so on. Suppliers also offered some applications packages, usually charging for them. With the advent of unbundling, led by IBM, more and more of the free software previously supplied must now be paid for, usually on a lease basis. This has put the manufacturers in a competitive position by opening the door to private companies that develop and market their own versions of systems software.

Software houses and consulting companies are the most active sellers of software today. A private software house usually markets a particular package in one of three ways. Having developed a system for a client, it may perceive its possibilities and generalize the system so that it appeals to other users. The original client may get royalties, a reduction in the development contract price, or both. A second possibility is that the package is offered to the software house by an independent developer, who gets a royalty on sales made. This is called "software brokering"; some companies specialize in it. Third, the house may develop the idea and the package independently, having decided that there is a worthwhile market.

Trade federations, research associations, and private industry are other possible sources of software. For example many of the early applications packages started off this way, a company may develop its own system to solve a particular business problem and then decide that it could be useful to others with the same problem. The package may then be offered for sale directly, through an industry group or through a software broker. Two other sources are user groups and government agencies. The development of COBOL is the most familiar example here; it was heavily supported by the U.S. government, the Codasyl Programming Language Committee (Association for Computing Machinery), and individual manufacturer's user groups.

Finally, many companies have been introduced to packages through a service bureau, which may acquire it in one of several ways. Users may pay to the original developer a royalty on each use of the package, ("publishing") with the service bureau providing all backup and support. Or the two parties may enter into what has come to be called a "piggyback" arrangement, with the service bureau acting as a wholesaler and with the developer providing support. Finally, the arrangement could be a combination of these, where the service bureau (or time-sharing bureau) offers the package for use in the bureau and pays royalties while at the same time the developer is offering it for sale. This gives the user several alternatives. He may start off by using the package via a service bureau and, as his processing load increases to justify it, swap over to running it on his own equipment. Or he may use the bureau to test the package before deciding to buy it. Or he may begin by buying the package and be assured of ready backup at the service bureau. This happy arrangement has been called, unhappily, "piggybackscratching."

Later chapters will cover in detail the guidelines for doing business with suppliers, the possible advantages and disadvantages that are inherent in the ways in which they develop and sell software, and important points that buyers should look for when negotiating the contract. The next chapter discusses the present circumstances of software availability from a historical perspective.

2 | THE HISTORY OF SOFTWARE

The purpose of discussing the history of software is to provide a perspective against which software advances (and setbacks) of today and tomorrow can be evaluated. In this survey, some of the important hardware developments must be mentioned also, for it is impossible to consider software without reference to its implementation. Programming and logic processing requirements have influenced computer designers just as much as the facilities and limitations of hardware have affected programmers and software designers.

THE INNOVATORS

If there is a theme in this chapter, it is that very little in today's software is really new. The basic concepts we apply now were developed before the first generation started, some of them before the first stored-program computer was even built. It is, however, a risky business to attempt to assign dates to the "first" use of any particular process, for two reasons. First, early programmers, although they may have documented their work, did not always publish it. It is almost impossible to trace back through the various versions of a compiler, say, to identify just when a particular idea was formed or incorporated in it; moreover, some of the earlier documents may no longer exist. Secondly, it is generally acknowledged that the technology for building computers existed for a number of years before the first work on them started. The impetus for computer applications was provided by World War II, particularly in the area of calculating ballistic missile trajectories. The work was naturally all classified. Groups in America, England, Germany, and Russia were working on computers quite independently of each other. Even in America, there were several groups developing computers who did not know of each other's work until

13

the war was over. It is not surprising that many basic programming concepts were hit upon by all these workers, without any group being aware of parallel work going on. Grace Hopper (34), who has been called the "mother of software," said recently:

> I was in uniform during the war; communications were limited and we worked under very heavy pressure. I did not learn about many things until long after the war was over. For example, I heard nothing of Dr. Zuse's work in Germany until long after the war was over, nor did I read Turing's paper until I had been in computers for some nine or ten years. . . . I did not meet Lovelace's work until ten or fifteen years later. . . . It is difficult to say who influenced whom. We were isolated. I was on a Navy crew. We were busy getting things done. At that time, we were not looking to what had happened, and we did not have the time to look at what was happening elsewhere. Not until 1946 did I have the opportunity of going from Boston to Philadelphia to see the ENIAC.

Grace Hopper's is the first of a handful of "famous names" that will be mentioned here. The names of her contemporaries are encountered over and over again in the lists of papers published in those pioneering days, and it would be impossible to compile even a brief history of computers and software without mentioning them. But, as they would be the first to point out, others not so well known today contributed just as much to the field. In more recent years, major developments have been announced not under the name of an individual but of large corporations, and even though the important concepts of these developments may be the work of only one or two innovators, their names remain unknown. When an individual is named or a "first" mentioned, therefore, these points should be kept in mind.

To avoid peppering the text with dates, and to provide an overview of the history of software, some of the key events are set out in chronological order in Appendix C.

Nineteenth Century Automation Developments

Among the early names that stand out in splendid isolation is that of Joseph Marie Jacquard, a Frenchman who invented a textile loom to weave intricate designs under the control of punch cards. The first version of his loom was burned by an angry mob of silk weavers. But Napoleon became interested in the device and it was soon declared public property. With government support, the loom became so successful, and brought such prosperity to Lyon that eventually a monument was erected to Jacquard on the very spot where the first loom was burned.

The Englishman Charles Babbage was not so lucky. At first he had a government grant for work on an automatic calculator, but as his plans got more ambitious, the money was withdrawn. Had he been able to build his Analytical Engine, incorporating logic processing worked out by the first programmer, Lady Lovelace, it would have been a true stored-program digital computer. A description of his machine differs little except in terminology from that of any modern computer. Its basic components were an arithmetic unit, working storage, a control unit, and input and output devices—punch cards and a printer. He envisioned three types of input: number cards (the data), directive cards (controlling movement of data in memory), and operation cards (instructions for arithmetic to be performed on the data). Further, he developed the ideas of conditional transfer from one instruction to another, based on the result of a "compare," and of "the machine eating its own tail"—looping on the basis of counters and changing previously set instructions. "A new, a vast, and a powerful language is developed for the future use of analysis, in which to yield its truths so that these may become of more speedy and accurate practical application for the purposes of mankind than the means hitherto in our possession have rendered possible." That was Lady Lovelace writing in 1842, and except for the style, it could be an advertising man's blurb for any third-generation computer.

And there the matter rested for almost a hundred years. In the late 1880s, Hollerith and Powers developed punch card equipment and established companies to manufacture and market it. Through a series of mergers, Hollerith's Tabulating Machine Company eventually became IBM, and the Powers Accounting Machine Company became International Computers, Ltd. At the time of World War II, however, they were engaged in the manufacture of punch card and accounting equipment.

Modern Computer Pioneers

The first electromechanical digital computer to go into operation was the Mark I, built during World War II at Harvard under H. H. Aiken. Grace Hopper (34), a midshipman at the time, was in charge of programming it. As she described it: "I wrote out a program, punched it into tape, took the ends of the tape, brought them together, used an iron with a little strip of gooey stuff and heat to make an endless tape, mounted it on a computer, set an assortment of switches, hoping they had been correctly set . . . pushed the start button and watched my program run." Although called by other names at that time, subroutines, list processing, and relocatable relative code were being used in this computer.

During the same years, engineers J. W. Mauchly and J. P. Eckert, Jr., were working on an electronic computer at the Moore School of Electrical Engineering at the University of Pennsylvania. Their first result was the ENIAC (Electronic Numerical Integrator and Computer), which weighed over 30 tons and had more than 19,000 vacuum tubes—and 20 words of internal memory. It was to take over calculations on ballistic missiles then being done on the differential analyzer. Eckert (24) described the advances in programming made, starting with the differential analyzer:

> To change a problem on that machine, one had to take a set screw driver, release the set screws on perhaps a thousand gears, remove these gears from the machine, figure out where a new set of gears should go, hammer on the new set of gears, try running the machine, find that some of the set screws were loose, tighten them up and make various adjustments, and, after about four days' work suitable for an auto mechanic, one would be ready to run the problem. In the original ENIAC we built, the setup was done by setting switches and putting in cords, rather like a telephone exchange. Once we had a diagram of what we wanted to do with this computer, we could go round with a couple of people working on the different switches and set up the switches and plug in the cords for such a problem in two or three hours. We thought we had made a vast improvement in the setup problem, reducing it from four days to four hours.

Even before the ENIAC was completed, the Moore School group began working on a new and much improved computer, the EDVAC (Electronic Discrete Variable Computer). Late in 1944 they were joined by the Hungarian mathematician John von Neumann, who concentrated on the logic and programming side. The functional specifications for the machine changed from day to day as it was being built. Von Neumann devised two sets of instruction codes for it and wrote a number of programs, including some to solve not a scientific problem, as might be expected, but the sorting of records into ascending sequence (39). At the end of the war the group broke up, von Neumann going to the Institute of Advanced Studies at Princeton with Goldstine, another of the original team, and Eckert and Mauchley going into business for themselves. Their company encountered difficulties later when the financial backer was killed in a plane crash, and they then joined Univac.

Back at the University of Pennsylvania, work on the EDVAC continued. Samuel Lubkin, among others, developed von Neumann's ideas for the final form of the EDVAC instruction set, based on a four-address system. The machine finally became operational in late 1951.

Von Neumann's classic paper, "Preliminary Discussion of the Logical De-

sign of an Electronic Computing Instrument," written with Burks and Goldstine at Princeton in 1946, covered almost all of the logic concepts on which
today's computers are based. For example, it discussed serial versus parallel
arithmetic, asynchronous operation, buffered input/output, subroutines, core
size, storage hierarchies, optimum word length, binary versus decimal code,
floating-point arithmetic, and the use of magnetic tape for high-volume data.
Von Neumann continued his work until his death in 1957, contributing
among other things the basic principles of sorting and merging, and flowcharting.

During the same years, a group at Cambridge University in England was also
building a computer. This one was called the EDSAC (Electronic Delay Storage Automatic Calculator). Like the EDVAC, it used mercury delay lines,
since vacuum tube flip-flops had proved uneconomical for stored programs. It
became operational in May 1949, the first operation of a stored program computer. It featured automatic address relocation and subroutine libraries. A
year later the first American stored-program computer was finished, the SEAC
(Standards Eastern Automatic Computer). The instruction set for the SEAC
included macros, although they were not yet called that.

An interesting historical footnote concerns the reasons why these new machines came to be called computers rather than calculators. As far as can be
determined today, several different groups decided on "computer" independently of each other, for different reasons: the word more closely described
the machines than the word "calculator"; it had three syllables as opposed to
four; and computers were taxed at a lower rate than calculators.

DEVELOPMENT OF SOFTWARE

First-Generation Machine Languages

After 1945 these wartime projects gradually terminated, but the scientific
and commercial possibilities of the new machines were well realized, and work
on them accelerated. As mentioned, Eckert and Mauchly were at Univac
(Sperry-Rand), where many of the ideas developed for the EDVAC were extended and improved. They were joined by Grace Hopper who developed the
first commercial programming language, FLOW-MATIC, for the Univac I and
Univac II. That language was the precursor to COBOL. Hopper also developed
the first commercial sort generator. Univac I was developed for the U.S. Bureau of Census, which had started Hollerith on his punch card equipment in
the 1880s.

IBM was not far behind. In 1948 it introduced the Card Programmed Calculator (CPC), which was not a stored program device, the instructions being wired in. However, it was popular, and filled a gap in the business world until true computers became easily available. Its floating point and three-address logic influenced later software development. First generation IBM 701's and 650's followed the CPC. The concept of symbolic addressing was implemented on the 701, using a Dewey decimal type of addressing on macros and sub-routines called in at compilation time. The programming language was an ancestor of the second-generation Autocoder, called SPEEDCODE. It appeared to the programmer to give the machine a three-address, floating-point instruction set with index registers, even though it was a single-address, binary, fixed-point machine. The popularity of the language alerted manufacturers to the higher priority that users gave to ease of programming over fast processing. The first 704's were delivered in 1956. They had the first FORTRAN assembler as well as the SHARE Association Programming (SAP) developed at United Aircraft. SAP allowed addresses to be programmed as a combination of symbols and decimal integers.

Interpreters were also used on the first-generation machines. These programs allowed simulation of one machine on another, bypassing the lengthy process of learning another machine language. Today, of course, it is technically possible to simulate any computer on any other, although it would be very slow and expensive. However, this was Turing's definition of the Universal Machine, published in 1936; it seems that we have achieved it without really trying to and without any real need for it.

Second-Generation Machine Languages

Second-generation computers began in 1959 with the delivery of the first transistorized machines. This was the same year in which the ATLAS was finished, work on COBOL began, and the great ALGOL controversy started to take shape. Each of these events leads us by a different path to the form of software today; therefore they will be treated separately.

FORTRAN and ALGOL

Some users, especially in the scientific community, were not altogether happy with the fact that FORTRAN was rapidly becoming the major mathematical programming language. It had been developed and at first almost entirely supported by IBM. The FORTRAN project team, headed by John Backus of IBM, had spent a reported 25 man-years developing the first FORTRAN compiler, which was delivered late and had a number of bugs. As with other compilers produced later, these bugs were gradually worked out, but not without a certain amount of grumbling from the users, as anyone who has attempted to use a new compiler will understand. The early FORTRAN compilers were slow, but they had a number of clever features. For example, an algorithm was included to analyze the flow of the program being compiled to optimize index register assignment. As programmers became more expensive and machine time decreased in cost, the philosophy gradually changed. Users wanted a fast compiler to compensate for the increase in the number of compiles needed during testing. Since, in a scientific environment, many FORTRAN programs were one-shot jobs, computer time to run the tested program could be a small percentage of the time needed to compile and recompile during testing. As a result, many of these optimizing features were dropped in favor of a faster compile time.

The next major revision of the compiler, FORTRAN II, permitted the use of subroutines compiled and debugged separately and called in by the main-line program. Use of the language spread rapidly. To compete with IBM, Philco, Honeywell, Control Data, and Bendix all announced computers that would accept FORTRAN source programs written for the IBM 704. Today, every major machine has a FORTRAN compiler.

Back in 1957, IBM was the major supporter of FORTRAN, and a strong one. Some users felt that it would be a good thing to have an algebraic language that was developed under the auspices of, and controlled by, the scientific computing community as a whole, not by a single manufacturer. Furthermore, they wanted a language that was hardware independent and that was not so clumsy as they felt FORTRAN to be. So, a group of 12 users met in Los Angeles in May, 1957, and signed a resolution directed at the Association for Computing Machinery (ACM), recommending that the ACM should "appoint a committee to study and recommend action toward a universal programming language."

The idea at first had generally widespread support, albeit some of it was lukewarm. For example, the chairman of the IBM user group SHARE called it "trivial." Official backing from SHARE was later withdrawn in favor of FORTRAN. The U.S. government did not support it, but neither did it come out officially against it. The ACM established an ad hoc committee for the "common algebraic language," which first met in January 1958. Enthusiasm was higher in Europe than in America; in fact, the European group GAMM (Gesellschaft fur angewandte Mathematik, i.e., Society for Applied Mathematics) had supplied much of the initial impetus. The next major meeting, six months later, was therefore held in Zurich. The result was a preliminary report on ALGOL 58 (the new language was also called IAL at first, for International Algebraic Language, but this was dropped in favor of ALGOL).

Initially there was general agreement on the basic features of the language, such as the notation to be used, but as the various subcommittees went on to advanced facilities like the manipulation of strings and storage allocation, there was a divergence of opinion. Several different experimental compilers were under development, each one embodying various subsets of the basic language. A number of new computers were announced with ALGOL-like dialects. All this diversification was contrary to the original aims of the ALGOL pioneers, but there was little they could do about it.

Early in 1960, the "Paris 13" met to produce another official set of ALGOL specifications. Originally 14 members were to meet, but one of them, William Turanski, was killed in an accident just before the meeting started. The ALGOL 60 report was dedicated to him. A few months later an experimental ALGOL 60 compiler was tested in Amsterdam and became operational that August. (It should be noted that ALGOL purists do not like to make the distinction between ALGOL 58 and ALGOL 60, saying that it is all the same.)

Interest in the language was strong in the United States for a few years, but FORTRAN had already gained such a strong position that there was never any real contest. In Europe the situation was different. In spite of the lack of good input and output verbs, ALGOL soon became the most popular language in academic and scientific installations and remains so to this day. Its proponents claim that it is the best programming language ever developed.

ALGOL has had many descendants. For example, the University of Michigan developed the Michigan Algorithmic Decoder (MAD) based on ALGOL 58. IBM's military computer language, the "Jules Schwartz' Own Version of the International Algebraic Language" (JOVIAL), as well as BALGOL and NELIAC, are others.

APL

Mention should be made of one of the newer of the scientific languages, called simply A Programming Language (APL). This was devised at Harvard by Kenneth E. Iverson, who needed a clear and precise way to describe algorithms, not necessarily just for computer processing. After joining IBM in 1962, he worked with Adin D. Falkoff and implemented APL there. Later, a number of time-sharing companies and universities adopted it, and C. J. Creveling at NASA-Goddard took a special interest in it. In 1970 a user's group was formed.

APL advocates, who have been described as "fanatics" and "nuts" because they are so devoted to the language, claim that it is easy to learn, and can handle vectors, matrices, and other arrays simply and powerfully. It is very flexible; a clever programmer can get dozens of operations into one statement, including input and output, although it does not have to be done that way. It does have some disadvantages, including an 88-character set of which 12 were especially invented for APL, and also needs a special typing head for terminals. But it does have the undeniable advantage of not having been developed by a committee and thus avoids the problems encountered with ALGOL.

Time-sharing scientific users have been putting pressure on their manufacturers to implement APL. Although it is still too early to forecast with confidence, APL will probably earn itself the number one position for its special
application area.

COBOL

Efforts to achieve standardization had somewhat more success in the area of
commercial languages. The United States government led off in May 1959
when Charles Phillips of the Department of Defense called a meeting in the
Pentagon of representatives from all the major manufacturers, some users, and
some government installations. The "carrot" was a hardware-independent business language, which users especially considered to be eminently desirable. The
"stick" was the government's determination not to buy computers from any
manufacturer who did not support the resulting language. The group in the
Pentagon agreed unanimously that such a language was both desirable and
feasible, and formed the Conference on Data Systems Languages (CODASYL)
and established short-term and long-term committees.

True to its name, the Short-Term Committee acted quickly. Representatives
from Burroughs, IBM, Honeywell, Univac, RCA, Sylvania, the Air Force, and
the Navy were included and soon formed two working groups, one to study
data description facilities and one to write procedural statements. Within three
months they had prepared recommendations for a full meeting. When these
were approved, they continued their work and published the first official report in June of the next year, although preliminary specifications had been released for general discussion some months before. The name chosen for the
new language was COmmon Business Oriented Language (COBOL).

Ideas for COBOL were drawn from many sources, including IBM's Commercial Translator system and AIMACO (from Air Materiel Command and Sperry-
Rand), but most of all from FLOW-MATIC. FLOW-MATIC included the concepts of detailed file descriptions with record and item definitions separate
from the procedure statements, and an English-language type of notation.
(But in the Univac I, a machine with less capacity than a medium-sized 1401,
FLOW-MATIC compile time was measured in hours.) An example of an instruction statement in FLOW-MATIC follows:

```
TEST EFFICIENCY (W) AGAINST .005;
IF LESS GO TO SENTENCE 27;
    AGAINST .01; IF LESS GO TO SENTENCE 28;
    AGAINST .015; IF LESS GO TO SENTENCE 29;
    AGAINST .020; IF LESS GO TO SENTENCE 28;
    OTHERWISE GO TO SENTENCE 27.
```

The item in parentheses referred to a file that had been previously defined. Compare that to a similar routine in simple COBOL:

```
IF EFFICIENCY LESS THAN .005 GO TO SENTENCE-27;
IF EFFICIENCY LESS THAN .01 GO TO SENTENCE-28;
IF EFFICIENCY LESS THAN .015 GO TO SENTENCE-29;
IF EFFICIENCY LESS THAN .020 GO TO SENTENCE 28 ELSE GO
    TO SENTENCE-27.
```

Immediately the teams began to line up for and against the new language. One of the first to object was the CODASYL Long-Term Committee, which had been studying the problem in a more leisurely and, as members contended a more objective fashion. They wanted to base COBOL on Honeywell's FACT, which had been developed on a contract basis by the Computer Sciences Corporation, a company set up for the purpose. The FACT language incorporated some of the same concepts on which the new COBOL was based and also borrowed some from FLOW-MATIC, but it went beyond the original COBOL recommendations. The FACT compiler reportedly contained 250,000 three-address instructions and required a minimum of 4096 words and 4 tape drives. The Long-Term Committee also said, with some justification, that COBOL had been thrown together in too much of a hurry and that more thinking was needed. The Short-Term Committee responded by saying in effect that the course of history cannot be reversed; their specifications were already published and "that was that"—which it was. Later revisions, however, did contain elements derived from FACT.

Other criticisms were sweeping statements that COBOL was too complicated, too inadequate, too oriented to certain types of computer, almost entirely developed by United States government and manufacturer representatives, and too inflexible. More specific attacks centered on the fact that no provision for punch card or paper tape I/O had been made, that the complete separation of the procedure and data divisions was undesirable, and that reserved words and character set were faulty (for example, that the character for a hyphen and a minus sign were the same). Many of these details were later adjusted. IBM was at first against COBOL, preferring its own Commercial Translator, but in 1962, due to user and government pressure, the company finally accepted it.

These preliminary CODASYL recommendations were also criticized for falling short of the original aims to produce a language independent of and compatible with all types of computers and "a standard method of writing a certain class of problem normally referred to as business data processing" with "everything in the language . . . *correct* English." Manufacturers began to produce versions of the COBOL compiler, but since the specifications contained both "required" and "optional" features, no two were alike. There were also differences between the American and European versions. It was not until 1968 that the International Standards Organization voted to accept the USASI standards. Although COBOL has not yet completely achieved those original aims, its adherents claim they are getting closer all the time. There is no doubt but that COBOL 61, COBOL 65, and other extensions and improvements have helped somewhat.

It seems unlikely that COBOL will ever be "finished," for CODASYL is still very active in recommending additions and extensions, and any user can submit suggestions. In 1969 and 1971 the Conference published reports recommending extensions for communications processing and character-string handling. At present, most of this kind of processing is handled by individually written software. The new recommendations would make this part of COBOL so that the programmer would not have to struggle with things like the conditional operation of programs for message processing, message handling, connecting and disconnecting terminals, and programmed security procedures to prevent unauthorized access to files. The facilities are divided into two sections, Data Description Language (DDL) and Data Manipulation Language (DML). Acceptance has been slow, and there is now doubt that the recommendations will ever be implemented. IBM and Honeywell are two of the principal critics, questioning not the desirability of the facilities but whether they can be made available to the user in a less clumsy form. Users who might otherwise campaign for CODASYL might switch to PL/1 instead, as will be discussed later.

In spite of its faults and the slowness with which improvements have been made, COBOL still has the distinction of being the closest language we have to a hardware-independent, universally compatible one. It has not suffered nearly so much as ALGOL from a proliferation of dialects, and it is the only successful commercial language ever developed by a cooperative effort of users and manufacturers. It has spawned a number of other software tools, notably decision table processors (TABSOL, DETAB-X) and report generators (RPG, NICOL) and it is the single, most widely used programming language.

Third-Generation Machines and PL/1

In late 1962, Thomas J. Watson, Jr., invited the top eight IBM executives to his ski lodge in Stowe, Vermont, to discuss software for the new System/360 range which was under development. *Fortune* magazine estimated that the total cost of the new series in the four years preceding its official announcement was $5 billion making it the biggest privately financed commercial project in history. Of that total, the original budget for System/360 software was

$125 million (58). Others have estimated the eventual software cost at any-
where from $200 to $500 million. Compare that to the $10 million annual
software budget for second-generation IBM machines, principally the 1400
and 7000 series.

In 1963, software plans had progressed to the point where the "Three plus
Three" committee was formed to draw up specifications for a new programming language. There were three representatives from SHARE, the scientific-
ally oriented IBM user group, and three from IBM. Their goal was to devise a
language that would combine all the advantages of FORTRAN and COBOL
while eliminating their disadvantages, providing a programming tool equally
suitable for scientific and commercial applications. The new language was officially announced on April 7, 1964, along with the System/360 range. The
technology of the new computers which justified calling them a new generation was hybrid integrated circuitry, which IBM called "solid logic technology"
—that is, transistors and diodes made separately and welded together. The
third-generation machine is usually defined as a combination of these hardware advances and new software techniques.

The language was at first called New Programming Language (NPL), but
British users quickly pointed out that it might cause confusion with their well-
known National Physical Laboratory, so the name was changed to Multi-
Purpose Programming Language (MPPL) for a few weeks, and finally to PL/1.

In 1965 the "Three plus Three" committee was expanded to include representatives from GUIDE, the commercially oriented user group. Its contribu-
tions to the specifications placed special emphasis on input and output.
Responsibility for development was given to IBM at Hursley in Hampshire,
England. The first compiler was delivered on April 1, 1966; as a number of
wits were quick to point out, April Fools' Day was a very appropriate choice.

First reactions were not good. Users seriously questioned the principle of a
general purpose language and said that far from combining the best features of
COBOL and FORTRAN, it was worse than either. For example, experienced
FORTRAN programmers protested loudly over the PL/1 requirement for very
precise directions to get a good compile, and compared it to FORTRAN compilers, which made use of "highly skilled powers of divination over the problems being solved, and are good at sweeping loose ends under the carpet."
Another big problem in the early days was the large number of bugs in the
compiler, which have since been corrected. Acceptance was slow at first also
because of conversion problems, a situation encountered with any new language. But pressure from IBM and a gradually increasing trickle of good reports from users have led to wider use.

Users report that training time, even for experienced programmers, is greater
than for older languages. A rumor current in England is that the first programmer who can successfully circumnavigate the world with PL/1 will have a

knighthood bestowed on him. But most admit that, once the break-in period is over, programs get written and debugged faster. Praise has been also given for its ability to handle file structures more advanced than COBOL will support (though not from lack of effort on the part of CODASYL, as previously pointed out). As of the time of this writing, there are no official non-IBM PL/1 compilers, but other manufacturers are expected to announce them soon.

Further advances included improvement to the PL/1 communications-handling facilities, and more are expected in the future. Also, some earlier users of full PL/1 were offered the use of two different compilers, one a fast version that produced relatively slow object programs and the other a slower version that gave tight, fast-running programs. More recently, IBM has announced official versions of these, calling them "optimizing and check-out compilers," also products of the Hursley center. The optimizing compiler is available for both OS and DOS. IBM literature says the Optimizing Compiler will

> "carry out a complete analysis of the program so that all possible paths may be recorded in 'flow units,' as they are called; thus the compiler can make reasonable decisions about the order of execution of statements and the allocation of machine resources, such as storage and registers."

(Sounds familiar? Look at the specifications for early FORTRAN compilers.) The feature requires extra compilation time, but can be switched on and off via parameter input. The check-out compiler is available only for OS and requires 100K bytes for best operation, twice as much as the OC, but runs much more quickly. It is primarily intended for on-off scientific jobs where fast compile time will more than compensate for slow execution time. At the time this is being written, it is too early to tell how these will be accepted.

OPERATING SYSTEMS

First-Generation Systems

Up to about 1956, most programming was done in decimal or octal machine language, in absolute (as opposed to relocatable) code, and with no library routines available. More advanced concepts were known, as previously mentioned, but their practical implementation for the average user had not then been achieved. Some were using a primitive assembly language that did little more than translate from decimal to binary on a one-for-one basis, with a "library" of prewritten routines available on cards to be included with the source or object deck at load time. Sorting of magnetic tape records, as some old-timers will remember, was done by transferring the records to punch cards, sorting the deck off line, and reading the sorted cards back in to be written to tape.

Early work toward an operating system began with the IBM 702-704-705 range. One "automatic programming language" (as they were then optimistically called) was Autocoder (later versions were developed for the second-generation 1400 line) for which the term "macro" was coined. The General Motors Research Center wrote a job monitor for the 704, and the idea of automatic sequencing of batches of jobs spread rapidly. With the advent of larger scale computers of this type, efficiency became more important. Users wanted to eliminate idle time due to human intervention for loading and logging programs and files, the necessity for operator action when a program hung, and the wasteful process of rerunning a job from the beginning when something went wrong; no restart facilities were available. Taking the operator and the programmer off line and using standard subroutines and symbolic device addressing became popular.

Second-Generation Systems

When the 709 was announced at the end of 1956 (it was basically a 704 with internally buffered I/O), a SHARE committee designed an operating system that eventually came to be called SHARE Operating System (SOS) at a cost of 50 man-years. It was at first not compatible with FORTRAN, but it did have features for source language modification at load time without the necessity for a recompile, and an advanced debugging facility. However, it was very complex, clumsy, and rigid, and was not a complete success by any means.

IBM's STRETCH and Univac's LARC were both introduced at about this time. Little is heard today about these giants because, to put it kindly, they were ahead of their time. Since they were somewhat similar in purpose, only LARC will be briefly described. It consisted of two independent computers sharing a large internal memory, I/O devices, and a processor-dispatcher for controlling input, output, and data transfers between them. They could be operated separately or as one unit when a large problem was encountered. Although both manufacturers had hardware problems, the principal reason for their failure was inability to get the software working properly. Only a very few ever went into operation.

Most of the early second-generation machines had as software a job monitor to control linkages between jobs, a low-level assembler, a compiler (usually for FORTRAN), a load program (usually bootstrapped in by the operator), a variety of subroutines and utilizes held on a library tape (mostly with absolute addressing so that the programmer had to avoid the areas where they would reside), and a core dump routine. It is thus easy to understand why there was a great deal of excitement when in 1959 a multiprogramming system was implemented on the ATLAS computer, built at Manchester University in England. The idea was not completely new, but its realization was a milestone. The single-level storage system allowed each programmer to act as if he had the entire memory available to him. With as little as 16K words, organized into pages of 512 words each, a program could be written as if it had available 2048 pages of virtual memory. Logical pages were brought in as needed from a high-speed drum. Another early practical multiprogramming operating system, called the Executive System, was developed by Honeywell.

Other advances in the first half of the second-generation included data channels, which allowed an I/O device to interrupt main-frame processing as well as overlap with CPU activities. The technique of writing the complex I/O routines to take advantage of this was beyond the capability of the average programmer. They were therefore prewritten, leading to the concept of permanently resident I/O supervisors to handle interrupt processing. Coupled with multiprogramming, interrupt processing created the danger of one program overwriting another's data areas or files, or intruding on another program, or skipping beyond its own input and reading in the next program as data. Monitoring facilities of the supervisors were therefore extended to protect against this. Command languages were developed to control the actions of the supervisors.

As the hardware technology improved and internal processing became faster, the delay in waiting for I/O became greater. The spread of multiprogramming was due to the need to utilize this lost time by giving one program a chance at the CPU while another was handling input and output. The technique was called "System Peripheral Output On-Line" (SPOOLING). The resident supervisors were enlarged to schedule the I/O, thus further decreasing turnaround time by doing away with queues waiting for a device to become available.

Improvements were also made in storage protect facilities in the later years of the second generation. In some cases, index registers were used, set to hold the upper and lower address limits for each program operating. Or, the register might contain a bit for each block or page of memory, indicating its status. Sometimes a flag would be stored in each word for the same purpose. Illegal use would cause an interruption so that the resident supervisor could take control away from the offending program.

Third-Generation Systems

The third generation brought little that was radically new in software. IBM, for example, talked a lot about its concept of "emulation," mostly in an attempt to soften up users for the changeover from their old machines, which had by then accumulated large libraries of successfully operating systems. The idea, of course, is closely related to simulation, and had been spelled out by Turing in 1936 and practiced by many first-generation programmers to avoid the tedious process of learning a new machine language.

At announcement time, IBM had also talked about a new type of operating system that would keep the computer working continuously at or near to capacity. Two years later, 31 operating system features previously announced were "decommitted." IBM had seriously underestimated the size of the software job. Furthermore, analysts and programmers who probably should have been assigned to the development of third-generation software were being kept busy supporting and modifying that of the Systems 1400 and 7000 series. When the situation was realized, large numbers of people were put onto System/360 projects. But it was a little late, and the panic situation caused what many users classed as poor-quality products. By 1966 an estimated 2000 IBM personnel were employed in programming and programming support, more than half of them on various versions of the operating system. One of the first released was called Basic Operating System (BOS), but a number of disappointed users preferred to stay with what had been intended as short-term stopgap, DEBE (pronounced "Debby"), which was nothing more than a hashed together set of stand-alone utility programs, but it had two supreme virtues: It was there and it worked. The acronym DEBE stood for Does Everything But Eat.

Another version of the operating system was designed for diskless users, Tape Operating System (TOS), but it was soon dropped from the preferred list. The first successful full-scale operating system was the Disk Operating System (DOS) followed by the Full Operating System (FOS), later abbreviated to plain OS. There are many differences between them, OS being the larger and more complex version. For example, DOS will support three-partition multiprogramming, whereas OS is geared to multiprogramming with either a fixed or a variable number of tasks, respectively abbreviated MFT and MVT. Also, the OS job control language is more extensive and very much more complex. Updates to the operating systems are issued at frequent intervals. They now work fairly well, but still cost what some users consider to be an inordinate amount of overhead.

Generally speaking, third-generation operating systems embody extensions of and improvements to features that were available in the second generation or before. The most important ones have been facilities to make data and programs resident on disk, drums, and/or tape, with the system taking over what had previously been programmer or operator functions. This was a natural evolution. Things like cataloging, buffering, communications with the console operator about errors and required I/O setup, internal initiation of I/O on a program request, invalid instruction procedures, and so on, are handled by the resident supervisor portions of the operating system.

The slowdown in development of new generations of computers has come as a welcome breather to most users, who are by now through the first hectic years of converting to the third generation. A "fourth-generation" machine is announced occasionally, but there have been no radical technological breakthroughs on the scale of the vacuum tube to transistor change, or from mercury delay lines to magnetic core memories. The problems with third-generation software have also led to a tendency to be wary of trading the devil we know for one we don't; at least what we've got now works. Further advances in software seem to be taking the form of improving on present systems, especially in the areas of real-time and time-shared processing. It cannot be denied that software has not kept pace with hardware and that the average commercial user relying on his manufacturer for almost all systems software is not realizing the full potential of his computer because of software deficiencies.

APPLICATIONS SOFTWARE

It is not nearly so easy to outline the milestone events in applications software. Recognition of the potential efficiency of packages has come not so much from the manufacturers as from private programming firms and the users themselves. The sale of, say, a stock control system by one user to another is not likely to be heralded with trumpets of publicity. There is no known historical record of the first systems analyst who, having just got his company's payroll installed, looked up and said, "Say, I wonder if someone would like to buy this?" It may have been, and very likely was, a payroll system, since rightly or wrongly (usually wrongly) this could have been the first one a new computer user tackled. It has been estimated that there are now more payroll systems in the United States than there are computers (31).

The interest in packages and the numbers of them offered for sale is directly proportional to the shortage of trained programmers and systems analysts. Their commercial success has, however, been limited by the fact that any one package is of interest to a relatively small market. They have been more successful in standardized industries, like banking and insurance, and less so in manufacturing companies, whose procedures are less likely to be similar to those of other companies.

The relatively small market for a specialized application package was what led to the development of generalized systems. Informatic's Mark IV, mentioned in Chapter 1, is considered to be the great-granddaddy of generalized processors; although it was not the first, it has been by far the most successful. IBM's Information Management System (IMS) should be mentioned, too (not to be confused with MIS, Management Information System). It has had a somewhat rocky history, but successful implementations should be on the way soon, if they have not occurred already. Much of the experience gained from the Bill of Materials Processor (BOMP) has been applied to it. Almost every other manufacturer has announced at least one such system, and some of them have several for different sizes and series of computers.

Recent years have also seen an increase in the numbers and types of programmer aids available. Some were mentioned in Chapter 1. These tend to be relatively low-cost packages, given little publicity other than advertising. Many of them were developed because of the bright idea of a programmer, who may have written the first version in his "spare" time and convinced his management it was useful; or by a programmer in a software house whose salesmen knew a good thing when they saw it; or as joint effort between a user and a software company. Reportedly, Applied Data Research, Inc., was the first to get a patent for one of these, which claimed 45 separate features of its AUTO-FLOW package. The patent took five years to process.

SOFTWARE
3 AS A
PROBLEM SOLUTION

This chapter considers the advantages and disadvantages of the major types of software available, as well as the reasons frequently given for using or not using them, and comments on the validity of these reasons, given the present state-of-the-art. Then, the use of software as the solution to a data processing problem is considered in the context of general systems development procedures, for software can be considered as a solution only after the problem has been defined. Even then, most of the steps leading to implementation of software will be identical to those of developing and installing an in-house system.

SYSTEMS SOFTWARE

The advantages of basic systems software and utility programs are widely known and accepted. It is hardly necessary to convince today's computer user of the benefits in using compilers, operating systems, sorts, and so on. Programming languages give a reduction in coding effort over writing in machine language, which is alone incalculable if only because it would have been impossible to find and train the required number of programmers to do the job in machine coding. Further, both low- and high-level languages give a tremendous degree of flexibility in comparison to what was possible on first-generation techniques. Debugging is infinitely easier and becomes more so as new features are added to compilers and assemblers. The amount of detailed logic design, especially for input and output operations, is reduced. Standardization is easier to agree upon and enforce, and even if this were only because flexibility was curtailed (a complaint often heard, especially from programmers discussing high-level languages like COBOL) it would still be a worthwhile trade-off. No one will argue with the point that less programmer training is needed. During the first generation and the early days of the second, before the proliferation of high-level languages and macro facilities, many commercial installations specified that their programmers must have, to start, a degree in mathematics. Also, the documentation produced automatically by today's systems software, particularly of programs, but also of machine usage, is improving all the time. Modern data processing as it is would be unknown without this type of software. So indispensable is it that it is meaningless to discuss disadvantages; we can, however, consider the major *faults* often attributed to current systems software.

Users complain of several inadequacies of available software, notably its inefficiency. As was pointed out in Chapter 2, it is evident that the power of systems software has not kept pace with that of hardware. It is a fair statement that in most commercial installations the full power of the equipment is never utilized because of the inadequacies of the software. Secondly, much of it is difficult to implement and use. Programmers attempting to learn the use of an advanced job-control language, for example, often require as much training as when learning a new programming language, if not more. Late delivery is another problem, but is not encountered so frequently, now that the major pieces of software for the third generation have been completed. Uses are becoming more wary, and future announcements from the manufacturers will be viewed, one suspects, with a grain of salt the size of a mountain. Stemming from the same causes are the problems of poor documentation and incomplete debugging, although the latter is now not so serious as it once was, and we have learned to live with the former.

These faults are not attributed to inherent defects in the software itself. They are due, to a large extent, to poor management and failure to realize the scope and complexity of the development problem faced by the manufacturers who produced the software. Some software was originally developed to be a sales aid for peddling computers, and that objective was obvious. Systems software is therefore amenable to improvement. As unbundling proceeds and manufacturers face serious competition from outsiders, the quality of the systems software offered can do nothing but improve.

ADVANTAGES AND DISADVANTAGES OF PACKAGES

Advantages

In the decision for or against the use of packages, there is considerable scope. The factors range from the long-range goals and general management philosophy of the user company at one extreme to details of a particular package under study at the other. These are summarized in Table 1. By far the most important benefit of applications packages, the one that alone justifies their existence is *reduction of programmer effort.* The proportion of system development time and cost spent on programming is a function of the complexity and size of the system, but is usually between 25 and 40 percent of the total. Savings to the user may run even higher than this if recruitment, training, and overhead costs are also considered. Further, it can be an advantage to have programmers available for work they would not otherwise be able to take on if they were coding the application by hand.

TABLE 1. THE PROS AND CONS OF APPLICATIONS PACKAGES

Positive Factors	Negative Factors
Less programmer time	Suitable package not available or can't be located
Less duplication of effort	
Faster implementation	Possible inefficiency
Superior product	Need for tailoring
Lower cost	Inflexibility
Lower maintenance cost	High capital outlay
Better support	Lack of support
Better documentation	Poor documentation
Staff freed for other work	Lack of acceptance in the installation

NOTE: Items appearing in both columns illustrate the fact that they are relative and can vary from one package to another and from one installation to another. These points are discussed in detail in the text.

Much of the cost of logic design is saved as well, but *not* that of the preceding steps (information gathering and analysis), as will be discussed in Part II. Another cost saving can be realized in the area of testing. First-level program testing is not required, although an acceptance/systems test is usually necessary. These savings, of course, result from the *reduction in duplication of effort* from one company to another and one industry to another, and in some cases from duplication of effort within the data processing department as the current year's programmers try to debug and rewrite last year's programs without adequate documentation. As Larry Welke (56) said:

> You'll find that in many, many cases, there are extremely busy, wonderfully talented and creative, high-priced people sitting back and reinventing the wheel time and time again. We don't make round wheels anymore, we make octagonal wheels and NO-OP the corners.

Another important justification of the use of applications packages is that very often the system *can be on the air sooner* than a handwritten one could. Whether the benefits are intangible and unquantifiable, or will mean direct cost savings and/or increased profits to the company, this early utility is usually to be desired. The only situation in which this is not true would be the one where the full delay is needed to install the input subsystem, convert the files, train staff in new procedures, and so on. This is rarely the case, however.

The package suppliers, particularly software houses, add other items to this list of benefits. They claim that *the user is getting not only a proven product, but one that is superior* to anything that he could produce himself. The "proven product" claim is not always true, of course. If it were, users would buy only software that others have proved, never giving a new package a chance, and that would be the death knell of the software business. The "superior product" claim has some merit. It is true, as the software houses claim, that the best technicians (systems people and programmers) tend to move to professional computer service companies and away from users when they discover that their career paths are strictly limited within the user company (if they wish to stay in data processing), and as they become bored with garden variety systems work. It is definitely not true that any system produced by a software house has got to be better than anything done in house.

On this subject, John Cook (20) said:

> The programs that have been developed *for* programmers *by* programmers—like Autoflow or Mark IV—are often more successful than the average application-oriented package. The computer-makers too have begun to realize, however faintly, that a gap exists between the elegant machine and the impressive list of applications packages and the needs of the real-world user. Some have begun to collect systems people and programmers with solid experience in business applications.

The lesson in this for the package buyer, which will be stressed in Chapter 6, is that he must investigate the background and qualifications of the developer of the package he is considering.

Users sometimes find that a package can be installed for a *lower initial cost.* However, it almost never happens that the total cost, including that of operating the system, is lower.

Other advantages of packages may be less maintenance effort, better support, and better documentation. This claim is usually justified. Maintenance may not be cheaper—in fact, it is very likely to be more expensive—but the user need not assign his own staff to the task because as part of the contract the supplier takes care of maintenance, at least for two or three years. This may cover both debugging and minor modifications to accommodate changes in the operating system, and so on. Major modifications needed because of changes in the business of the company, in user procedures, or for legal reasons can usually be handled by the package supplier for a price, so that the user again need not reassign his own programming staff to deal with it. "Support" covers such things as training, file conversion and implementation assistance, and forms design. How extensive this is will vary, and should be negotiated before the contrast is signed. The documentation *should* be better than what is produced in house, on the average, but isn't always. It is up to the package buyer to evaluate the documentation offered and determine whether it is adequate. Evaluation criteria for documentation will be given in Part II.

Finally, software houses are always quick to point out that by buying a package, *installation staff are freed to work on other projects.* However, sometimes the claim is that the programmers thus released can devote their time to the bread-and-butter systems of the company while the package takes care of more esoteric processing. At other times, the opposite claim is made, namely, that if a package to handle ordinary processing is purchased, the staff are then available to work on the more interesting and experimental systems. Of course one argument might apply in one installation and the other in another, or both might be applicable in the same installation at different times in its history, depending on the backlog of work, level of the staff, and the data processing needs of the company at that time. The point to note here is that the decision on whether to buy a package, and if so which one, must be taken in light of the known capabilities, interests, and ambitions of the data processing staff, as well as the availability of recruits.

Disadvantages

The list of benefits to be derived from the use of applications packages is impressive, and would seem to accelerate their use rather than to create the aversion so evident in the past few years. However, from the viewpoint of potential users, disadvantages can outweigh the advantages. The most frequent shortcomings are discussed next.

Availability

One user, deciding for several of the reasons given previously that he would buy a payroll package rather than write a new one, set up a project team and very systematically and professionally began to gather information on packages suitable for his particular configuration. Thirty-five different ones were identified. After a detailed study, it was found that only one met all the requirements—but after all, one was all that he needed. The most interesting point is that the acceptable one was not on the original list of 35, and was found only by sheer accident. The system has now been in operation for some time and the user is more than pleased with it, thanks to a chance discovery. The story illustrates what is probably the single biggest difficult for the potential package user: *ignorance of the existence of a suitable product.* There is no single software clearing house, no catalog, no service that can provide cheaply a list of *all* possible packages for a particular application on a particular machine. There are many sources of information, and the user may have to consult a number of them to develop a list of potentially useful packages, but even if he does this he never knows whether he has missed what could be the best one of all. How to go about looking is covered in detail in Part II, and a list of some of the sources of information is given in Appendix B. The task is still a difficult one, however, and it does not seem likely that a remedy will be forthcoming in the next few years at least.

A reason frequently given for failure to use a package is that *none is available*. As just indicated, however, it is very risky to make such a statement, even after an investigation; there might be one in operation right down the road that was (understandably) missed by the investigators. When this reason is given, it should be translated as "We couldn't find one" or sometimes as "We have never heard of one so we didn't even bother to look." If this is the *only* reason for not considering a package, it is not a justifiable one. The search process, as will be described in Part II, is not so exhausting or expensive as to be prohibitive, and can often be accomplished within a perfectly reasonable budget and timetable, viewed in relation to the potential savings that might result.

Efficiency

Another negative reason frequently given is that a package is *inefficient*, because it is generalized and not specifically written for the particular circumstances and requirements of the job in hand. There is no conclusive, objective evidence available to either prove or disprove this argument. One wonders, though, just how efficient the average *hand-tailored* system is. Given the expertise of the average systems analyst and the average programmer in user installations, coupled with the panic atmosphere in which so many systems are written, it is more than likely that many user-written systems are very inefficient indeed. Any clumsiness of a generalized system, supposing that it does in fact exist, may in many cases be more than offset by the expertise of the systems designers and programmers who worked on it, coupled with the profit motive for producing a better mousetrap.

Tailored Requirements

A more valid objection may be the need for tailored features. The user may be presented with the alternatives of changing his business procedures or altering the package. The former course may well be unjustifiable, while the latter could cost as much or more in programming and machine time as writing the system from scratch. Suppose that the data processing department is asked to provide an automated system for a certain user department—let us say the accounts department for the purposes of the example—and upon investigation finds that quill pens and nineteenth century business procedures are still in use there. Suppose also that the department has on hand a really "superduper" little package, available cheap from the We Never Sleep Software House, incorporating the latest accounting practices. Should the user be forced to change his procedures, which admittedly are inadequate anyway? The proper answer to that depends on the answer to another question: Would the procedures be updated even if the package were *not* used? If the answer to that is yes, then this is one of the few instances where one can recommend that the user change to fit the computer system rather than the other way around. In fact, the best answer would probably be to effect the changes on a manual basis before automating them. Regardless of whether it is desirable, however, it is not always possible to change business practices, and the need for tailored features can be a very real one and a major stumbling block to the use of a package.

Inflexibility

Related to this is the possible inflexibility of a packaged system. This is especially true of packages originally written for another company and then either picked up by a software house or marketed directly by the original user. "We treated it gently and operated it only on alternate Fridays" is *not* a selling point for software. There may well be no options to suppress unneeded files or processing, for example, or to inhibit unwanted reports or generate on-demand-requests. Again, modifications to provide extensive options may cost more, and will almost certainly be more trouble, than if the user does it himself from the beginning.

Cost

The capital outlay required is sometimes given as a reason for not using a package. Unless the installation is in a situation where programmers would otherwise be idle, however, it is rarely true that writing one's own system is less costly when a feasible package is available. The lump-sum price of the package may *seem* higher because it is more visible; costs of developing systems in-house are not only spread out over a larger number of items and a longer time-span, but may well not include all the true costs. How many installations, for example, calculate the cost of training of systems staff for a new project, or of recruiting to fill gaps left by turnover during the project, when costing a new system? Yet these expenses will not be incurred, or will

at the least be considerably reduced, if a pre-written package is used. Some
software houses cannily take into consideration the average sum a data processing manager can spend on a single item without higher authority, when
pricing their packages.

Support, Documentation, and User Acceptance

Lack of support is a valid complaint in a few cases, particularly if the package was developed as a system for another user and made available publicly
only as an afterthought, if the seller is another user anxious to recoup some of
his development costs without too much trouble, and sometimes if the seller
is a service company but *not* the original developer of the package. It always
pays to investigate the history and pedigree of a package. Who were the origin-
ators, how good are they, and are they available now and in the future to service their brainchild? Sheer geographical distance between the user and the
developers can be a problem, which is unfortunate because it limits international exchange of techniques and systems that could otherwise be very
useful to the industry as a whole. Only the biggest software houses and manufacturers can afford to guarantee full support on an international basis.

Often coupled with lack of support is poor documentation. Debugging a
system written in another company is bad enough, but without adequate
documentation, training, and testing help it can be impossible. The same
holds true for modifications. Software houses, however, are often reluctant
to provide full details of the programs because of possible threats to the security of their product. The user must ask himself if he really needs such
complete documentation for his own systems; if the package includes full
maintenance, he may not.

Finally, there may be lack of acceptance of a prewritten package. This is
more often encountered within the data processing department than from the
user. Richard Canning (15) called this the Not Invented Here Syndrome (NIH)—
that is, "If we didn't develop it, it can't be any good, and we're not interested
in it." That argument in itself is specious, but it is true that it may be difficult
to retain good programmers who are assigned to maintaining someone else's
system, more so if that someone else is an outsider. Further, the installation's
programmers may be losing very valuable experience that could have been utilized in future systems. This problem can be partially reduced if one or two of
the best programmers—the ones most valuable to the installation—are assigned
either to help evaluate the package or, if this is too dangerous because their resistance is already established, assigned to understudy the system with the supplier. Initial reluctance may be overcome as the programmers become involved
with interesting new ideas; if this introduction is successful, a little extra insurance can be provided by having in house at least one person thoroughly familiar with the detailed workings of the system. Each manager will have to
judge for himself whether this is a workable idea in his own installation.

Some of the points made above lead into a discussion of the policy of the installation in relation to the purchase of software.

INSTALLATION POLICY

Before a yes-or-no decision on the particular use of an individual software package can be made, data processing management should examine the company policy and the aims of the installation to determine what guidelines they offer concerning the use of packages in general. If a particular philosophy has not been established in certain areas, or has not been formally stated, it should be formulated and documented before any software shopping expedition is undertaken.

For example, attitudes of management that would obviate use of an outside package, or at least restrict such usage to very complex items, (i.e., systems software) would be a policy of building the reputation of the installation as an advanced data processing user leading the field in innovation. If general history and policy of the installation is to recruit high-grade experienced staff, and/or to build the expertise of the systems and programming staff through outside and on-the-job training to a very high level, then packaged software probably will not fit in with this attitude.

Also, some companies and some industries, such as the oil industry, are traditionally wary of cooperative ventures of any kind and are reluctant to let onto the premises any outsiders who might also have contacts with other companies in the same field. A package supplier is quite likely to have such contacts. A business such as this, which relies to a large extent on trade secrets to maintain an edge over the competition, is not a likely candidate for applications packages.

Some companies, on the other hand, have as a positive policy the attitude that cooperation with others in the same business is a desirable thing. Insurance companies are a good example, and in fact they frequently trade or sell home-developed systems to each other. A company with this policy is more likely to want to use packages if possible.

Another management attitude that should persuade the data processing manager to adopt the use of packages is that of giving the user the best possible service as a top priority. This is often coupled with extreme cost consciousness so that a package appears obviously to be the best solution.

Traditionally, the data processing department has a monopoly; users wishing to have their business procedures automated must go to them, and must pay whatever costs result, either directly or indirectly. Some companies now take the attitude that this can lead to unnecessarily high costs and that it is

economically advantageous when their own data processing department has
some competition. One of two principal methods can be used. One is to require the data processing department to prove, by getting outsiders to bid on
the job, that they can do it more cheaply. The department has a built-in advantage in that it does not need to make a profit on its activities as computer
service organizations do. The other approach leaves it up to the user to get
the cheapest deal he can, and he is perfectly free to go to an outsider if he can
get the same quality product at a lower cost than the bid the data processing
department has put in. In either of these situations, both user and data processing department should consider the use of applications packages almost
every time.

A further incentive to buy a package is management's decision to level off
the number of personnel employed in systems and programming or to reduce
them. A very large project might require, it the work were to be done in house,
a buildup of staff to twice or three times the normal level. If management cannot see future projects that would require an increased level of staff, they may
be reluctant to hire them for the short term. And even if they are willing to do
so, it might not be possible to get the qualified staff required when applicants
realized the limited tenure of employment. A software package, installed "as
is" or even with major modifications, might be the answer in this case.

Finally, a package should be seriously considered when time is short. Compliance with legal requirements, changes in the company's business caused by
an acquisition or merger, dynamic changes in the company's marketplace or
competition, or sheer short-sightedness on the part of management can all
bring about an urgent requirement for a new computer system. A package can
very often be on the air faster than a handwritten system ever could.

Examination of these points of installation policy and the environment in
which systems are being developed should be made before any or all packages
are considered—in fact, before any systems development work takes place at
all. They should be reexamined at regular intervals to see if any changes have
occurred, or if any changes are needed.

HOW SYSTEMS ARE DEVELOPED

Most readers are probably familiar with the process by which computer systems are developed. This discussion is a review, with special attention paid to
how the implementation of a software package differs from that of a system
fully developed in house.

The selection of software cannot be carried out independently of the business environment in which it will operate. The exercise is not an academic or

technical one, but a business project. The evaluation, selection, and installation goes through the classical systems development cycle, with software examined as only one of a number of possible solutions, or as a part of the total solution.

A generalized diagram of the problem-solving loop is given in Figure 3. It begins with a definition of the problem, goes through information gathering and problem analysis steps, to implementation of the solution, and finally to a reevaluation of the solution to see if it really solves the problem. The reevaluation may well occur after a time lapse; circumstances can change, so that an adequate solution may become worthless after some months or years have gone by.

The iterative nature of the process is important, which is why it is called a "loop." Note that there are three decision diamonds in the diagram, each one introducing the possibility of a return to a previous step. The first one asks whether the problem has been defined correctly; if it does not, more work on it is needed. An attempt to find a solution will be a waste of time and effort if the problem was not defined correctly in the first place. Analysis of the problem is then required; it may be found at this point that there is insufficient information to proceed, which again causes a return to a previous step. Finally, after a solution has been sketched out, it is tested (either in reality or as some form of simulation) to determine if it will work. It should be tested again after implementation to see if it is *still* working. Note that a negative answer to the question "Have we found the best solution?" can lead right back through the two previous decision diamonds in Figure 3 to the beginning of the loop.

The system development cycle, diagrammed in Figure 4, is a specialized version of the general problem-solving loop. It is shown here with nine major steps. Most lists that one sees of the steps in the process include documentation as a separate step; in fact, documentation must occur throughout and really cannot be considered to be a process that can be defined in isolation from the others.

Software may be considered as a solution only after the problem has been defined. The application selection step, therefore, will almost always have been accomplished before any software package has been located or examined. Just as the attitude that "we've got a computer, what shall we do with it?" is a hallmark of sloppy management, so is that of "we've found this package, what will we implement with it?" At a point early in the process it will have been decided whether the problem requires a broad-scope solution cutting across several application areas (i.e., a management information system or company-wide data base) for which new systems software (and perhaps new hardware) or a generalized file processor might be considered. The alternative problem is one of standard systems design and programming, limited to one application

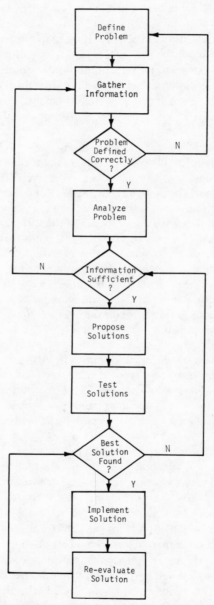

FIGURE 3: GENERALIZED PROBLEM SOLVING LOOP

area, for which a possible solution might be an applications package. Or, the problem might be one internal to the data processing department. An aid is needed for documentation or debugging, for example; or the problem might be one of installation management or creating a good technical environment for programmers. Regardless of the nature of the problem, it is still necessary to go through a problem definition (application selection) and feasibility study stage. The computer user in this context might be any department of the company, a section within a department, including data processing, or several departments together; it may even be top management as a group.

The result of the application selection process will be some kind of a statement defining the problem area and possibly defining the problem itself, at least in part. In an ideal world this will be documented in the form of a user request or systems proposal (the actual name of the document is unimportant.) Or, as sometimes happens, it may be a memo or even a verbal brief to the systems analyst, asking him to "have a look at so-and-so." He must then perform some kind of feasibility study. Again, in a perfect world this will be a formal study going through the stages of information gathering, analysis, final definition of the problem, and the design of an *outline* system to answer it. In fact, he should propose several outline solutions, giving the costs and the benefits of each, for a management decision. In some companies, however, particularly for a relatively small-scale project, the process may be considerably condensed to the point where a formal feasibility study is not performed at all—the analyst sleeps on it, checks on the unused capacity of the installation's disk files, and says "yes, we can do it." More and more managers are learning, however, that such a compromise study usually leads to disaster.

The most important part of the feasibility study (or system investigation, or preliminary design, or whatever it happens to be called) is the *definition of objectives,* what the problem solution must accomplish. The objectives usually fall into one or more of the following areas:

Increased profits
Cost savings
Curtailment of an otherwise inevitable increase in costs
Reduction in staff
Better management information
Better service to customers
Compliance with legal requirements

These objectives must be explicitly stated and *quantified whenever possible.* If this is not done, it will be impossible to judge which of several proposed solutions is the best, and after the system is implemented, management will not even be able to judge its effectiveness—whether in fact the company has got

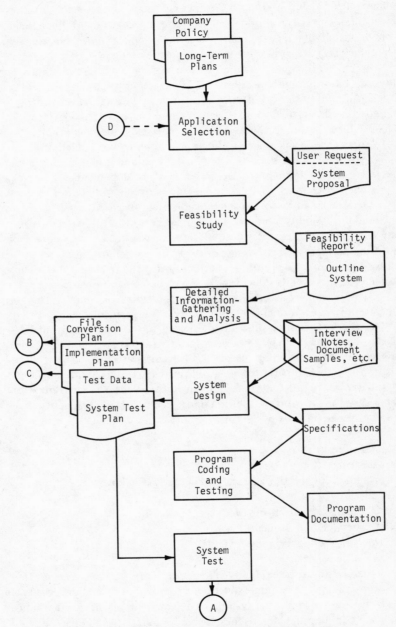

FIGURE 4: THE SYSTEMS DEVELOPMENT CYCLE

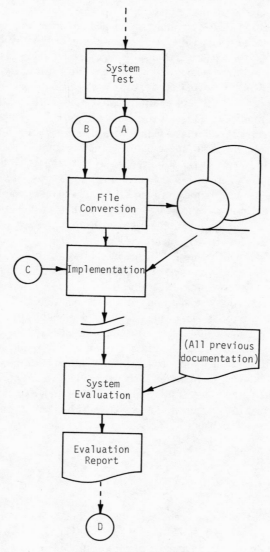

FIGURE 4: (continued)

its money's worth. How the statement of objectives is used in evaluating possible software solutions is discussed in detail in Part II. A suggested outline for the study is given in Chapter 4.

After the problem has been defined and the objectives stated, solutions can be proposed. They may range from "do nothing" to a revision of manual procedures to a full-blown computer system. The advantages and disadvantages of each should be set out in the feasibility report by the systems analyst, with his recommendations. Each possibility is weighed against the predefined objectives before making a decision. At this point, one of the possible solutions could be to "look for a package to do it for us." The process of package location and evaluation then becomes a further feasibility study. Or, the evaluation may be part of the original study, so that a decision to go ahead with it means that the company then is committed to buying software. How the evaluation is actually carried out is the subject of Part II.

It should be remembered that a feasibility study is a *risk venture*; the money budgeted for it should be not more than 15 to 20 percent of the total cost of the system up to the day it is put on the air. This means that if a software package is purchased, about 8 to 12 percent of the *purchase price* alone (leaving aside extras such as training and modifications) is a reasonable sum to devote to the initial study. If the package is leased, then a calculation of the annual rental multiplied by the number of years of expected life of the system will give the base figure from which to work.

A number of difficulties present themselves, however. First, software prices vary widely and the purchase price may bear no relationship to the actual value of the system to the company. Secondly, the price to be paid will not be known until *after* the study has been completed and the decision made. The figures given above, therefore, are only rough guides and should not be taken literally. The point being made is that if a negative decision be made, there may be no return at all on the study, and therefore it is wasteful to spend a great deal of money on it. The rule of thumb usually given is that a feasibility study of even a major system should take no longer than eight to ten man-weeks. That assumes that extensive travel is not required, and that an experienced senior analyst is assigned to the project. Allowance must be made for individual circumstances and staff capabilities.

SYSTEM DESIGN

Let us suppose that it has been decided to go ahead with a computer system, whether it is a package or a homemade one. The next step is detailed data gathering, requiring the analyst to go out into the user department, interview both management and workers, get samples of all documents presently used, and obtain other pertinent data. This process will be only slightly curtailed if the new system is to be a package, for it will still be necessary to design input procedures to get data from the source documents into the computer system, the area where the user is most closely involved.

System design must take place too, but it is at this stage that the advantages of a package begin to be realized. Design need encompass only the input and possibly the output subsystems; the files and programs, of course, will already have been worked out by the package developers.

Program coding and testing is completely eliminated if the package is to be installed "as is," or if the supplier has agreed to take on modifications himself. If the user installation intends to modify the package, then time and money must be set aside for it.

Preparing for and conducting file conversion and systems testing (for a package it is usually called *acceptance testing*) will be just as costly and as time consuming for a package as for an in-house written system, but probably not more so. The same is true for implementation. The primary difference in these steps may be that outside assistance is available from the software supplier, somewhat reducing the amount of effort required from the installation staff.

Finally, evaluation of the working system is even more essential for software than for in-house systems. It is the only way to determine whether the company has obtained value commensurate with the cost of the analysis. Further, it can provide valuable lessons for the future. If the evaluation concludes that changes are needed so that the system can continue to meet the original objectives, the analysis may lead to a decision to rewrite the system. Depending on the scope of the changes, rewriting will lead back to more information gathering, system design, and so on, or even back to a new feasibility study if the proposed modifications are extensive.

Because the life span of a computer system, whether or not it is a bought package, is usually five to seven years, the system development cycle is seen to be an iterative process, as is any problem-solving loop.

PART TWO | # THE EVALUATION

4 | PLANNING AND INITIATING THE PROJECT

A brief overview of the systems cycle was given in Chapter 3, with emphasis on the feasibility study. With that as an introduction, this chapter returns to the initial feasibility study and the tasks in the early stages of the project, including establishing the project team, scheduling, and locating possible packages to do the job.

THE FEASIBILITY STUDY

As was mentioned, the decision to go ahead with a computer system is usually based—or should be based— on a formal study of the user's requirements and problems and possible methods of meeting them. This may be called a feasibility study, a systems proposal, a system definition, a statement of objectives, or any one of a dozen other names. Its title is irrelevant but its contents are not. A suggested outline is given in Figure 5. It is not the purpose of this book to present documentation standards; in any case, such standards should always be developed for the particular needs and environment of each individual installation, not adopted wholesale from a book or package of standards. The outline serves to illustrate the kinds of things that should be included in the study. If standards for this type of document do not exist, then the suggested contents in Figure 5 could be used for guidelines in preparing them.

It was stressed in Chapter 3 that the most important part of this document is the statement of objectives, quantified wherever possible. Table 2 illustrates the kinds of objectives usually set for computer systems, which can be expressed in terms of getting something *faster, easier, more,* or *better* in return for *less* of something else. Or, the improvement desired may be more subtle;

51

I Introduction

   Scope of Study
   Boundaries and Constraints
   Methods Used
   Terms of Reference
   Acknowledgments

II Outline of the Existing System

   Environment
   Functions
   Major Files and Documents
   Problem Areas

III Statement of Objectives and Requirements

IV Outlines of Proposed Solutions

V Costs and Benefits for Each Proposed Solution

VI Recommendations

VII Outline Plan and Schedule for Implementing Recommended Solution

Exhibits and Appendices

FIGURE 5: AN OUTLINE OF A FEASIBILITY STUDY

for example, it is rare for a computer system to actually *reduce* the number of personnel needed. What may happen is that there will be a curtailment of an otherwise inevitable increase in staff. The quantification should be expressed in actual figures or percentages. For example, it is not good enough to say the system should achieve "a reduction in the percentage of out-of-stocks." What percentage? Percentage of what number of orders? Number of items held in stock? A better statement is ". . . a reduction in out-of-stock items from the present level of XX% to XX%" (whatever the figures are). Or, another example: *not* "saving in clerical staff" but "to limit the increase in numbers of new staff needed to not more than one new clerk per year, as opposed

TABLE 2. SYSTEM OBJECTIVES

Faster, Easier, More, Better	For Less
Money (income, profit)	Money (expenditure)
Accuracy	Staff
Timeliness of reports	Time
Service	Paper
Management information	Work
Flexibility	Worry
Compliance with legal require- ments	

to the present growth rate of three per year, which would otherwise be ex-pected to continue at that rate."

Almost all objectives can be quantified in some way, although not neces-sarily in money terms. It may well be impossible to put an exact figure on the profits to be gained from better service to customers, but the better service it-self can be quantified, for example, in terms of reduced turnaround time in answering customer queries, or fewer inaccurate invoices, or faster turnaround time between receipt of order and delivery of the goods. These items should be quantified in hours, percentages, and other precise terms if money values cannot be attached to them. (How to handle this type of objective when doing a cost/benefit analysis is discussed in Chapter 8.)

It is always wise to have the user department management review the study and formally approve the statements in it, appending any modifications or alterations they would like to make after discussion with the systems depart-ment. It is then possible to go ahead with a reasonable degree of confidence that major changes will not be required later. No system, however, is com-pletely static, so changes in the company and the business areas concerning the user may require changes to the specifications of the system even before it is implemented. A certain amount of this is inevitable, and the greater the time span between the approval of the study and implementation of the sys-tem, the more likely it is that changes will be required. If for some reason there has been a delay after the feasibility study, a review with the user should be held before the project is restarted.

It will be assumed from this point that the user, management, and the sys-tems department have all agreed that a problem exists for which a computer solution is indicated. It will be further assumed that a software solution will be one of those considered, usually along with the possibility of doing it in-

house. In this context, the "user" may be the data processing department itself if, say, systems software or a programmer aid (for example, a flowcharting package) is under consideration. The next steps will be:

1. Assign personnel to the project.
2. Establish a schedule.
3. Locate possible packages.
4. Begin collecting information on the packages.
5. Establish the criteria against which the packages will be judged.
6. Prepare the feature comparison check lists.

Obviously, a number of these steps can proceed concurrently. Preparation
and use of the feature comparison check lists will be discussed in detail in
Chapter 5, and examples will be given. This chapter covers steps 1 through 5
in the preceding list. (A more detailed task list for the software selection
project is given in a later section, "The Project Schedule.")

SOFTWARE SELECTION PROJECT TEAM

The first step in choosing the person or persons for the project is to consider the skills and abilities required, which will vary according to the nature
of the project. Most of the necessary attributes, though, will fall within the
following areas:

1. *Hardware:* knowledge of the machine to be used, peripherals, etc.
2. *Software:* knowledge of the operating system, machine language, programming language(s).
3. *Application area:* familiarity with the business area, users environment,
results of the feasibility study, and so on.
4. *Techniques:* skill in documentation, report writing, costing, decision
tables, and so on.
5. *Team leadership:* ability to manage own work and that of others.
6. *Personal:* tenacity in searching out facts, thoroughness, objectivity.
7. *Experience* on similar projects.

The relative importance of each type of attribute will depend on the project.
The best approach is to list the necessary attributes in order of priority and
then consider those among the available staff who best meet the requirements.
Weak areas can be strengthened in one of several ways. If, for example, one
person meets all requirements except experience in this type of project, a more

experienced person could be assigned as his "advisor" (not a full-time job), thus not requiring that the second person be released from whatever other job he is on. Or, if the lack is in the area of hardware, software, or techniques, consideration should be given to extra training for the individual before the project begins. A weakness in any of the high priority areas, and especially in the ability to manage a team (even if it is only a one-man team) signals a need to soften the schedule.

If the project as a whole falls into any category rated higher than trivial, it should be managed by a senior systems person. He should be able to draw on user personnel, operations staff, and experienced technical people within the data processing department, as necessary. It is almost always a mistake to put a technical person such as a programmer or a systems programmer in charge of selecting an applications package. Because of his training and natural inclination it may be very difficult for him to maintain the necessary degree of objectivity. His interest will inevitably be centered on the technical details of the software rather than its commercial applicability. That is not to say that such a person is not needed on the team; he may be one of its key members. But his technical bias should be balanced and should be overridden as needed by consideration of the user's requirements and the economic facts of life.

There are three prime requirements for a *user liaison* person attached to the project team. First, he must have authority to make day-to-day decisions without having to clear them with his own management. This probably presupposes that he is at management level within the user department. Secondly, he should be thoroughly familiar with the application area under study and should know not only how the present system works, but also how it may be affected by business trends and future requirements. Last, he should have a basic knowledge of computers. If he has had no previous exposure to computer systems and the data processing department, a short introductory course on computers (say, a week) and/or study of an introductory text is a minimum requirement. If this basic education is omitted, data processing people on the project team will find it necessary to educate him themselves, thus slowing down the work. (Of course, in most companies the task of user education does fall to the data processing department. But it should be a separate task; otherwise, it will inevitably be overlooked in preparing project schedules. This is one of the most common factors in failure to meet a system deadline. Even *after* the fact it may not be recognized.)

If time is critical, the key people should be identified so that some provision for backup can be made should the worst happen. Experience has shown that the worst *does* happen from time to time; there are any number of reasons why a team member may become unavailable, ranging from his resignation to an emergency appendectomy or worse. At the very least the manager should have a mental list of people who could replace him if necessary. A better arrangement would be to appoint understudies who are responsible for keeping themselves up to date with the project so that if they are needed no time will be lost on orientation. This will require that the understudy spend a small portion of his time away from productive work, the price to be paid for the insurance.

THE PROJECT SCHEDULE

The same basic principles apply to establishing a schedule for a software selection project as for any other type, with some special points for care. The amount of time and effort spent on the schedule will depend on the scope of the project, and could range from a half-hour outlining the major tasks and pencilling in the approximate amount of time allocated for each, to several days in working out the various task assignments and getting approval from management and user. Even for a small-scale project, however, some kind of a schedule should be set, to prevent the exercise from turning into a never-ending search because it is interesting, or conversely, to ensure that the dull steps are not "forgotten" or skimped so that appropriate emphasis on each task is assured. For a large project a schedule is essential to keep the work within reasonable limits of time and budget; and as a learning tool, to consider in retrospect how actual times compare with what was planned, where did it go wrong, and how can it be prevented next time.

The steps are: draw up a list of tasks, assign individuals for each task (if it is larger than a one-man project), estimate man-time for each step, and finally assign calendar dates for completion of each stage. With a little practice and a well-organized approach, this can be done quite rapidly. A sample task list for the selection project is given below. For a big job the tasks shown can be broken down further into smaller units; for a small one, some may be omitted or combined.

1. *Phase I*
   Finalize assignments and schedule.
   Review feasibility study.
   Establish selection criteria.
   Locate possible packages.
   Collect information about each one.
   Prepare feature comparison check lists.
   Estimate nonstarters and draw up a short list.
2. *Phase II*
   Review and adjust schedule for succeeding steps.

Obtain more detailed information about possibles.
Study possibles and prepare summary sheets.
Arrange and carry out discussions with suppliers.
Visit user installations.
Perform cost/benefit analysis.
Perform technical evaluation.
Arrange and carry out test runs.
Make final selection.
3. *Phase III*
Negotiate contract terms.
Have legal department review contract.
Sign contract.
Finalize plans for installation and acceptance testing.

In Phase I, it may be difficult to assign *elapsed* times to some of the steps with any degree of confidence because the team may be dependent on waiting for replies to letters, setting up meetings, and so on. More comments will be made about locating possibles and the other steps in this phase later in this chapter and in the next.

Phase II plans should be reviewed at the start and adjustments made in assignments and expected times required for each task, depending on how many packages remain on the list, whether a technical evaluation is needed for each one, and so on. Preliminary estimates may be made in Phase I, but these must be refined when the number and nature of the packages on the short list for in-depth study is known.

Phase III tasks may be very brief or they may be lengthy (although not necessarily requiring a lot of time from data processing department staff), depending on the size of the package and complexity of the legal arrangements. The last task on the list refers to installation of the package and acceptance testing. This should be treated as a separate project, with a separate set of plans and schedules drawn up for it. Part III of this book covers the considerations for Phase III tasks in detail.

LOCATING POSSIBLE PACKAGES

Finding the "possibles" can be one of the most difficult and time-consuming tasks of the whole project, especially if attacked haphazardly. No single source can be guaranteed to produce all possible packages for the problem area. Set out a plan of action and allow plenty of elapsed time for the search (although actual man-days required may be low). Several lines of search can be followed simultaneously. Those mentioned below are set out more or less in the recommended order of battle, taking into consideration cost, time, degree of difficulty, and likelihood of success.

The Computer Manufacturer

. At the least, this first step will turn up the software offered by the manufacturer himself. If the salesman or other contact is knowledgeable and cooperative, he may be able to put the analyst in touch with independent suppliers or other users who can also help. The manufacturer may be the *only* source for big items of systems software, such as compilers, but as unbundling proceeds the private software houses may offer them competition. Thus it is advisable not to stop with the manufacturer, but to seek out these houses and even *other* manufacturers as a last resort. The policy of competitive manufacturers toward nonusers of their equipment varies from very cooperative to downright hostile, but contact with them could uncover something with which to compare other packages or even a package that could be purchased outright and modified.

Software Catalogs

There are a number of catalogs and they range in cost from free to very expensive and in level of detail from a two-line listing of any and all software submitted to a selective and comprehensive analysis. Those that supply the most detail and prescreening are, of course, more expensive. Most are available on an annual subscription basis with an updating service. The better ones may be an excellent investment for large installations that, as a matter of policy, buy a lot of software. The small company looking for a one-time package probably will not find the big, expensive services worth the price. A number of these catalog services are listed in Appendix A, with prices and addresses to which a firm may write for more information.

Software Houses

These fall into three groups: companies that develop and offer their own software for sale, either as an exclusive activity or as an adjunct to other service activities such as contract programming or consulting; brokers who sell (and may or may not themselves maintain) software developed by others, who may be a software house, a user, a private group or individual, a university, etc.; and service bureaus who offer the package for use on their own machines as part of a complete service and sometimes for use in house as well. They may be tracked down through the literature (below), or inquiry letters may be sent out wholesale.

The result of mail inquiries will be a flood of sales literature, some of which will be related to the problem. This literature should be studied for "possibles" to put on the list, and more information can be requested if necessary. Salesmen may call also. There is absolutely no obligation to see a salesman who is calling "cold" without making an appointment. Some companies may offer to make a presentation to describe their product. The best policy is to postpone these visits until all possibles have been located and the more likely ones chosen. It is a waste of time for all concerned to sit through a lengthy sales talk only to discover that the software will not be ready in time, will not fit on the available hardware, or just does not meet the requirements, when all this could have been determined from a sales brochure. Request documentation instead at this stage.

Search of the Literature

Hundreds of data processing periodicals are available. These can be inexpensive and very fruitful sources of information about software. First, there are the advertisements; second, many of the magazines have as editorial content a section on new software products that have been announced; and third, there may be feature articles by users describing their experiences with a package. Appendix A lists some magazines that specialize in software. A systematic search should include some of these as well as a representative selection of general data processing magazines, going back for two or three years (at least in those that have been published for that long). This search may mean scanning, say, 200 issues. The job is not so formidable as it sounds; it is easy to learn where in the magazine to turn for the "new software" columns, and the advertisements are usually on the same pages or close by. If one is not sidetracked by irrelevant material, the whole job can be done in two or three days at the most, or less for a fast reader.

Few user companies, however, subscribe to all these periodicals. Anyone in or near a large city can easily find back issues of magazines at the business periodicals branch of the public library. Some manufacturers maintain good libraries that a user can get permission to visit. Also, try any of the data processing associations the company or individual staff members may belong to. As a last resort, a friendly computer salesman or consulting company may be contacted; the staff of these companies often need to consult back issues of periodicals and can tell you where to find them.

There are also abstracting services that survey all data processing periodicals and publish magazines with one-paragraph summaries of the articles. These abstracts are available by subscription or, again, can be found in a business library. However, they cover only feature articles and therefore are of limited value in this type of exercise.

Consultant Service

Many data processing consultant companies will take on a software search and selection job. Before approaching one, determine how much of the job they will be asked to do—a list of possibles, a short list, or the complete job up'to and possibly including contract negotiation and supervision of the software installation. The advantages of hiring a consultant include freeing the installation staff for other work, and possibly expediting results because the consultant service will have more experience with this type of job, contacts within the industry, and possibly a head start from information already in its own files. For a major job, outline the requirements to several companies and ask for proposals on how they would conduct the job, how long it would take, and how much it will cost. Reputable consultants do not charge for making a proposal of this kind.

The proposal should include a statement of how much time the consultant's staff intends to spend in the company studying its requirements, both in the application area and the data processing department. This could range from a few hours if the job is to present a bare list of "possibles" for a stock control system to many months if they are able to make the final selection of a large, generalized file processor. Taking those two extremes as examples again, the cost might range from a few hundred dollars to $50,000 or more. A fixed-price arrangement is preferable to a time and materials one.

Choose the consultant carefully. In particular, a good reputation, familiarity with the application area and/or the hardware to be used, a proved record of completing work on time, and a professional, well-organized approach are more important than past experience in selecting software, although that would be a plus too. Avoid companies who sell their own software or appear to be pushing a particular package before they are thoroughly familiar with your requirements. They should *not* get a commission or any other consideration from the software supplier. A consultant who recommends his own company's software may, in fact, be offering the best deal, but it is impossible to be absolutely sure of his objectivity. If that software is really the best for the job, an independent evaluation will come to the same conclusion.

Other Users

Other companies that have had experience with the software may be contacted through computer user associations and/or trade associations to which they belong. There are two possibilities here: that someone else has installed software of the type you are looking for and can put you in touch with the supplier (as well as give their comments on it; see Chapter 6), and/or that a company has developed its own system and would be willing to give it to you, sell it to you, or arrange a swap. Also, there is an outside chance that someone else may have done a similar search and will be willing to let you have the information he collected. That, however, is to be considered in the category of manna from heaven.

A competitor can be particularly valuable in specialist areas like insurance, banking, and publishing, but be sure first that company policy allows such contacts with the competition. Then write to the data processing manager of each company on the list with a simple statement of the type of package required, hardware limits, and any special circumstances. Be prepared to reciprocate. This method has the advantage of being cheap and fairly quick, but it can be used only as an adjunct to a comprehensive search of the literature or a good software catalog.

If there is good reason to believe that there are packages "out there" somewhere that would fit the job, but other measures have failed to turn up a satisfactory assortment, writing to a data processing magazine with a request to be published in the letters' column might be considered. Most software suppliers scan the letters' columns regularly to find prospective customers this way. Or, another user may respond. Finally, word of mouth may help; perhaps one of the installation's employees knows about a package from a previous job, or a chance acquaintance at a data processing conference or exhibition might suggest a contact. But again, these sources are not the primary ones, and should not be totally relied upon.

For a popular application like payroll, stock control, sales analysis, or flowcharting, the sources suggested above will yield a fat list of "possibles." In fact, it may have to be curtailed to prevent the evaluation from becoming an enormous task. But what if the application or the circumstances are unusual, and the search turns up nothing even remotely likely after a reasonable amount of time and effort has been expended? There are a number of possibilities. Develop the system in house or, if that is too expensive, shelve the project or drop it in favor of a noncomputer solution—no further comment is called for here if one of those is chosen. Or, consider a joint venture with another user to share the development costs. Or, get a software house to develop the system for you and then make it available for sale to others to defray the costs. How much can be saved this way depends on the marketability of the system. Some suggestions for negotiating this type of arrangement are discussed in Chapter 9.

Documentation of Sources

As the possibles are identified, documentation of each one can be collected. A sales brochure and/or an outline description of the system should be sufficient at this point. It can be an imposition on the supplier as well as a waste of the project team's time to obtain a full set of documented specifications before it has been decided whether further study is warranted, especially if there are more than two or three packages on the list. The kind of information that will be needed for the first round of study falls into the following categories:

Identification: name of package, name and address of supplier.
Operating information: number of programs, time cycle.
Technical data: programming language, hardware configuration.
Functions: reports produced, files, main processing.
Availability: delivery lead time, price, terms.
Special notes: any unusual features or requirements.

This information will be used for preparing feature comparison check lists. Chapter 5 contains a detailed discussion of what information is required and gives examples of how it is used.

ESTABLISHING SELECTION CRITERIA

The process of acquiring software is analogous to making any other major purchase. Consider the example of buying a car. Most people have a mental list of requirements before they begin looking, whether or not these are articulated. On the top of the list will be the primary purpose—that it can get the owner from one place to another. Most people know whether they want a family car or a sports car, and they will have a top price in mind. Other considerations may be trade-in value for the old car, finance terms, age, country of manufacture, availability of parts, mileage averages, and so on. In fact, these things will determine not only what car is purchased, but who it is bought from. This, of course, assumes that emotional factors will not affect the decision to purchase.

Software acquisition is a business transaction and should be an entirely objective process. The factors against which the software is to be judged should be established in the early stages of the project, *before* any study of possible packages takes place. It can be done while the search is in progress rather than before it starts, however, because there will be inevitable delays while waiting for replies to letters or other inquiries. The list developed need not be lengthy or elaborate, but it should be documented. Special requirements should be included, but in general there will be four main categories:

1. Features: These are based on the objectives and requirements as set out in the feasibility study, which should be reviewed before starting this exercise.

2. Technical and operational data: All data pertaining to maximum core size, configuration, maximum computer time (daily, weekly, monthly), any limits on new forms, and other operational requirements must be stipulated.

3. Implementation and maintenance: Amount of support needed from the supplier, whether complete documentation is required or if some can be pro-

duced in house if necessary, any known future modifications due to planned changes in the user department, and similar specifications are delineated.

4. Price: Price should be expressed as an annual figure so that later it can be compared against either rental price or outright purchase price divided by expected number of years of use, subject to the usual discounted cash-flow allowances, and so on. If in doubt, the company accountants should be consulted for help.

A simplified example of a selection criteria list for a flowcharting package, based on the preceding list, is given below. Note that all possible features or facts about the package are not specified, but only the minimum requirements it must meet to be seriously considered.

Features
Accepts COBOL and FORTRAN source statements as input.
Permits detailed and summarized flowcharts as desired.
Vertical format.
Mainline high-lighted in some way.
Loops shown on one page.
Cross reference to source program.
Suitable for use in debugging as well as documentation.

Technical and Operational
Accepts input from cards or disk.
Fits in one 30K partition.
Will handle any number of jobs without need to reload.

Implementation and Maintenance
Available immediately.
No training needed; instruction manual for programmers should be self-explanatory.

Price
Not more than $2000 a year.

The selection criteria list is to be used both in developing a short list for further study and as a starting point for an in-depth study. Without it, there will be no objective measure of the software options being considered and the evaluation will be at best subjective and at worst blind chance. If this step is minimized or done poorly, the results may be a completely useless purchase and a great deal of wasted money.

EXCEPTIONS TO THE FORMAL SELECTION PROCEDURE

The object of this book is to set out a formal procedure for finding and selecting software. For most purposes, a formal, well-organized method of comparing one package to another and comparing each one individually to the
user's requirements will give the most satisfactory results.

In most cases it is desirable to investigate all possibilities in order to be sure
of finding the best one. But, as with any standard procedure, there are bound
to be situations that call for exceptions in which the formal steps outlined here
can be modified or even omitted altogether. For example, a software salesman
may call on the data processing manager and offer him a nice little debugging
program at a low price. Perhaps up to now there has been no need for it because no one knew the aid was available, but it is easy to see that, by using
the product, programmer time in debugging will be reduced and the task made
easier. Suppose further the procedure is easy to use, requires only a minute or
two of machine time per compiled program under test, costs $200 or $300,
and the salesman guarantees satisfaction or money back. To insist on conducting a full-scale search and selection would be silly. It is obvious that any rival
product, even a free one, would be *more* expensive after the evaluation cost
was added in, perhaps several thousand dollars more (hardly worth it) and
could not possibly offer a compensatory improvement if it were at all similar.
The decision is a yes-or-no one, and should be made quickly.

On the other hand, there are some situations where an abbreviated form of
the selection study is worthwhile even if software is not one of the solutions
under consideration. Take the case of a fast-growing chain of supermarkets in
England whose management wanted to install a computerized inventory control system. It was a new and necessary venture for the company because no
formal inventory control procedures were in use up to that time, not even
manual ones. For reasons of prestige, top management decreed that the system *must* be developed in house. The systems department was at a loss at first
because no one in the company had a good knowledge of inventory control
procedures. A study was therefore conducted; this involved training key people
in basic inventory methods *and* studying a number of applications packages
that were designed for inventory control. The researchers studied the data
processing magazines for "possibles," obtained sales brochures from suppliers,
and developed criteria lists and feature comparison check lists for the packages. All this information formed the background for developing specifications
for their own version of a system. It also served as a basis for comparing actual
development costs with package costs after the system would be on the air.
This comparison was presented to management which, as a result, agreed to
consider packages for future systems.

5 | THE FEATURE COMPARISON CHECK LIST

The initial steps of evaluation and selection projects were discussed in Chapter 4, including ways of locating possible packages, getting the basic information needed for each, and establishing the selection criteria. To review briefly, the selection criteria will usually fall into the categories of software features, technical and operational considerations, implementation and maintenance, and price. Within each category, there will probably be upper and/or lower limits defining the acceptable solution.

ORGANIZING CHECK LISTS

As the sales brochures and other sources are collected, it is necessary to organize the material so as to provide a quick check that all the basic facts are on hand, to provide an easy method of comparing one system to another, and to evaluate each "possible" against the basic selection criteria just established. The check-list approach has been found in practice to be the most convenient way of doing this.

The mechanics are simple. Basic items of information about each package are listed side by side under the appropriate headings. The features covered should include all those on the selection criteria list, plus any others common to the type of software being studied, along with identification information. They are best described with examples.

One example is given in Figure 6. This is a real-life case, the comparison of operating systems being part of a larger equipment selection study. In this case, the operating system was only one of a number of pieces of software studied for each computer. In the final selection, the system considered to be the best for the installation was only one of a large number of factors associated with the hardware.

Name	System A	System B	System C	System D
Job initiation, loading, etc.	Yes	Yes	Yes	Yes
Job accounting	Optional user-written routines	Yes	Yes	Limited
Utility routines	Many	Some	Some	Some
Operator communications	Yes	Yes	Yes	Yes
Job I/O control	Yes	Yes	Yes	Yes
I/O Monitoring	Yes	No	Yes	Yes
Complete protection	Yes	No	Yes	Yes
Job priority scheduling	No	Yes	Yes	No
Multiple job stream	No	No	No	Yes
Multi-programming	Yes	No	Yes	Yes
Maximum number of simultaneous users	4	1	7	6
Roll in/ Roll out	No	No	Under operator control	No
Remote job entry	No	No	Yes	No
Typical core residency	100K bytes	12K words	3K words	20K bytes
Minimum practical core	128K bytes	65K words	65K words	65K bytes
Typical system overhead	10%	0.5%	Nil	Nil

FIGURE 6: A FEATURE COMPARISON CHECK LIST: OPERATING SYSTEMS

Note: The suppliers' names have been omitted from Figure 6 and from most of the other examples used throughout the book. The features and capabilities of most software change from time to time in response to requests from users, or to extend or improve the system. Computer users will know that this is particularly true of operating systems. These changes are too rapid to allow definitive descriptions to be published in book form, for they would probably be out of date before publication. Even descriptions in magazine articles cannot be relied upon to be always up to date. In any case, no single list can provide the relevant information for many different companies and their needs. These feature comparison check lists are presented as examples of the *type* of information needed and its documentation.

Figure 7 is an example feature comparison for decision table processors. It illustrates the types of information needed for a quick comparison. Note that each of the features listed can be described in a few words. The list is set up in such a way that the information can be entered as a simple yes or no, or as a figure, or in a few descriptive words. This example is also drawn from a real-life study of decision table software.

It is more difficult to give examples of applications software. The lists of possible features for each of the many application areas served by package software would be much too lengthy for this book, and in any case could not be guaranteed to be completely comprehensive for all possible users. Instead, Figure 8 is merely a check list for the types of information that might go on such a feature comparison list. Not all items would be needed for all packages. The application area will itself suggest additional entries. Everything mentioned on the criteria selection list (see Chapter 4) should, of course, be included.

Figure 9 is an example of a feature comparison check list for computer control and accounting packages, one type of application package for which the user would be the data processing department itself.

Figure 10 is a partial check list for generalized file processors (again condensed from a real-life project). In fact, more than a dozen packages were on the original list, with about two dozen key features listed for each one. This was a major project for the company, since more than six man-months were used just in locating the dozen packages, studying the literature, and preparing the check lists, which were backed up by brief narrative descriptions of each system. The narratives concentrated on the use of the system from the point of view of various application areas, and the advantages and disadvantages of each one for the company. Three of the systems were then chosen for further study.

Name	Detab-65	360 DLT	S/360 Macros	Tap
Supplier	IBM	IBM	CSI	Hoskyns
Output language	COBOL	FORTRAN	Assembler	Assembler
Type	Pre-processor	Pre-processor	Macros	Pre-processor
Conditions	50	99	6	19
Actions	50	99	16	19
Rules	99	64	16	32
Rule test type	Condition test	Condition test	Rule mask	Condition test
Sequence of rule identi-fication	As input	Optimal	As input	By precedence
Table format	Vertical	Vertical	Vertical	Horizontal
Table type(s)	Limited only	Limited and extended	Limited only	Limited and extended
ELSE rule	Required	Optional	No provision	Required
Diagnostics				
Contradiction	Y	Y	N	N
Redundancy	Y	Y	N	N
Completeness	N	—	N	N
Format	Y	Y	N	Y
Price; terms				
Further study recom-mended?				

FIGURE 7: A FEATURE COMPARISON CHECK LIST:
DECISION TABLE PROCESSORS

Package name	File creation
Supplier name and address	User program
Name of contact, telephone	Procured package
number	File maintenance
Developer (other than supplier)	User program
History and place of use	Procured package
Equipment required	File security
Programming language	System usage security
Type of system (brief	Control, backup and recovery
description)	features
Type of logical file organization	Expansibility
Principal access method	Maintenance procedure
Record length restrictions	Modification procedure
Record format restrictions	Types of documentation
Type of input	Training requirements
Media	Availability
Prepared by	Price; terms
Options	Further study recommended?
Standard output	
Output options	
Data retrieval options	
Operating environment	
Teleprocessing	
Time sharing	
Multiprogramming	
Core requirements	

FIGURE 8: A FEATURE COMPARISON CHECK LIST
FOR APPLICATIONS PACKAGES

In the sample task list for the project, given in Chapter 4, the sequence of steps first established the selection criteria, then located possibles and gathered information, and then drew up the feature comparison check list. In fact, it is usually necessary to work on these tasks more or less concurrently. Study of the information collected will suggest additional items to put on the criteria list, which will result in an addition to the feature list and may in turn require the gathering of more information about the other packages.

Name	Package A	Package B
Supplier	Company A	Company B
Equipment	360/30 and up, DOS	360, OS/MVT
Job scheduling	Up to 3 partitions; extensive	No
Job control	Via operator	Resident module
Job Accounting		
Meter time	Yes	Yes
Clocktime	Yes	Yes
By peripheral	Yes	By type
By item quantity	Yes	Limited
Off-line costs	Yes	Yes
User budget balance	No	Yes
User invoices	Can be programmed	Yes
Multiprogramming	Yes	Yes
Tape and disk control reports	Yes	No
History file produced	Yes	Yes
Machine utilization statistics	Yes	Can be programmed
Contract terms	Indefinite lease	Indefinite lease
Availability		

FIGURE 9: A FEATURE COMPARISON CHECK LIST:
COMPUTER CONTROL AND ACCOUNTING PACKAGES

USING THE FEATURE COMPARISON CHECK LIST

The most immediate use of a major feature check list is for verification that all necessary basic information has been gathered. It is obvious that a blank will be quickly spotted. It insures that gathering and documenting of the information proceeds in a speedy, well-organized manner. When this round of information gathering is completed, the check-list format makes it relatively easy to eliminate the obviously impossible packages. It is merely necessary to compare each package to the selection criteria list and cross off those that fail to meet specification. If, for example, the terms of the project require that the

Name	System A	System B	System C
Company	Company A	Company B	Company C
Type of equip- ment	360/50 and up	Any (sic)	GE
Programming language	User language	User language	COBOL
Type of system	Retrieval and operating system	File manage- ment and operating system	File access and program com- piler
Logical file organization	Inverted	Hierarchical	Determined by user
File structure	Random	Random	Random by page
Information storage type	Fields	Tables	Records
Information related by	Dictionary	Dictionary	Chain pointers
Record length restrictions	None	Not applicable	Fixed within type
Basic access method	Direct	Direct	Direct
Physical re- trieval	Dictionary look-up	Dictionary look-up	Random to page, seq search to mast, chain to detail
Retrieval by content	Via dictionary	Via dictionary	Must be pro- grammed
Operating en- vironment	On-line, TP, MP, and TS	On-line, TP, MP, and TS	Batch; TS on 600 series
Data base inde- pendent of program	Partially	Yes	No
File creation by system	Yes	Yes	No

FIGURE 10: A FEATURE COMPARISON CHECK LIST:
GENERALIZED FILE PROCESSORS

Name	System A	System B	System C
File mainten- ance by system	Yes	Yes	No
Security	Terminal, pass- word, and by data element	Terminal, pass- word, and by data element	By record type
Usage statistics	Yes	Yes	User-written routines
Backup and recovery	Procedures built in	Many options	None
Availability	Operational in pilot	1 year	Operational

FIGURE 10 (continued)

new system use present equipment, any package needing additional hardware can be eliminated; packages which at first glance seemed possibilities may turn out to be deficient in the required processing; or, one or more may not be available by the deadline established.

It may happen that *none* of those on the list meets all selection criteria. In that case, the analyst will have to review the criteria to see if perhaps they were too restrictive. The check list makes it easy to find in what areas each package is failing; if one or more may meet top priority criteria, the suppliers could be contacted to see if modifications are possible. Or, more important, the analysis may indicate that software is not the answer to the data process- ing problem; then alternate solutions suggested in the feasibility study, such as doing it in house, can be investigated without spending more time and money on the software alternative.

If only one package of obvious merit is left on the list, the remaining tasks in the project are simplified. A more detailed study will still be necessary in most cases, however, to verify the quality and suitability of the software, the supplier, and the contract terms. The exceptions would be small-scale pur- chases like programmer aids, whose importance do not justify more expend- iture on evaluation.

The ideal number of packages left for the short list is between two and six. If there are more than this, the detailed study will be very lengthy and almost never be worth the time and effort because it is likely that one of the two to six packages will do the job just as well. A final choice can be made by refining the selection criteria to eliminate all but one contender. As an alternative, an additional list of features, in more detail this time, can be drawn up as an intermediate step between the quick comparison and a full-scale, in-depth study. The check lists in Chapter 6 suggest items for inclusion on the second list.

WHEN ONLY ONE PACKAGE IS BEING CONSIDERED

It may happen that only one package is left on the list or that only one to do the job could be located. Or perhaps the software is not essential and justifies only a "yes or no" decision. Programmer aids and one-of-a-kind software supplied by the manufacturer may fall into the last category, especially if the installation's equipment or configuration is unusual.

In some cases, it may be wise to go back to the package-locating phase and spend more effort to find other possibles. The study might be more productive if it included a dollar/value comparison of similar software designed for other machine systems. Whether or not a detailed study and technical evaluation are carried out with only one "possible" depends entirely on the type of package and the individual requirements of the installation.

SUMMARY

Preparing the feature comparison check list is a relatively short and easy step in the evaluation study, but it is an important one. It provides the short list and the starting point for information gathering necessary for a more rigorous evaluation, and produces compact and easy-to-use documentation of the major items of information collected up to this point in the project.

6 | THE IN-DEPTH STUDY

With the initial round of information gathering completed and the list of "possibles" narrowed down to a manageable number of "probables," the time for detailed study of those remaining has arrived. The remaining steps leading to the signing of a contract for acquisition of the software are:

1. Detailed information gathering and study.
2. Technical evaluation.
3. Cost/benefit analysis.
4. Preparation of the evaluation report.
5. Contract negotiation.

The pros and cons of a technical evaluation and the various methods of conducting one are discussed in Chapter 7. Chapter 8 covers the cost/benefit analysis and the final report for documenting and presenting the results of the study. Contract negotiation is discussed in Chapter 9. Each of these steps depends on detailed information gathering. In this chapter, the methods of getting the required information are presented, along with guidelines on the kind of information needed, especially that for a critical evaluation of the features and characteristics of the software and the software supplier. At this point the user is concerned with the questions: Will this package meet our requirements? Is the supplier a company we can confidently do business with? The subsequent chapters cover the questions of operating efficiency, value for money, and contractual commitments and guarantees.

ESSENTIAL ELEMENTS OF THE STUDY

The scope of the detailed study and the time spent on it are entirely variable, although the study is not expendable. The following factors determine the extent of the analysis:

1. The number of systems to be investigated: This comprises those left on the list after the first elimination round based on the feature comparison check lists (probably two to six).
2. The complexity of each system: It is more than likely that for any given project the packages to be evaluated will be nearly equal in complexity, but for different kinds of software they may range from very simple to very complex.
3. The importance to the company of the system: Even a rather small system in terms of costs and operating time might be critical to the profitability of a division or, indeed, the whole company. It may thereby warrant much more care in selection than a larger system whose failure would not have disastrous consequences.
4. Ease of getting information: This in turn depends on who the supplier is, how old the package is, geographical considerations, and so on.

Take, for example, a job-control language generator that would be used only within the data processing department and would give marginal benefits (in terms of the total operating commitments of the department). Obviously, the lack of this package could be regarded as unfortunate but not crippling, and would therefore justify less time and energy spent in research and evaluation than a generalized file processor for a companywide data base, even though the same absolute number of systems might be available for each one.

For the study, the sources of the required information include:

The developer, from his documentation, informal discussions, and through formal presentations.
Published literature.
Other users.
Direct data, i.e., by a demonstration of the system.

It is by no means necessary to employ all these sources. Which ones are chosen depend on the package itself as well as on the planned scope of the study and ease of access and organization. The considerations for each of those possibilities, types of information to be gained from each, and special points to look for, are discussed below.

The kinds of information to be sought out are also not foreordained, but

will depend on all the factors previously mentioned. The check lists and recommendations given later in this chapter should not be taken as defining the
actual limits of the investigation, but the maximum possible limits. Some
kinds of information depend on the type of package, others on its complexity
and the urgency and potential value to the company, as has just been discussed. The check lists must be tailored to the particular problem in hand.

The importance of planning project tasks in advance was stressed in Chapter
4. That stricture is doubly important for this stage of the study, for it is in
the information gathering that the temptation to go further and further and
to do more and more is greatest. While every small item of data that will be
required cannot be known in advance, it is possible to specify the methods
and areas for investigation and to specify the resources (time, money, and
manpower) to be spent on the exercise. The investigation may otherwise
turn into an endless process.

SOURCES OF INFORMATION

System Documentation

If the developer and/or the supplier is a software house or manufacturer,
the minimum amount of information supplied (in addition to the sales brochures) should be a detailed product description, including standard contract
terms; input and output samples; and operating instructions. Complete documentation of the system may well be required, and what it should show is
detailed later in the chapter.

The supplier should also be willing to answer specific questions and/or to
make available an experienced consultant who knows the system well. As a
rule of thumb, the more expensive the package, the more information you
can reasonably ask for and expect to get. Therefore, not much can be expected if the package is inexpensive or free, although there should be at least
a summary description and program documentation. If this basic minimum
is missing or poorly done, the wisest course is to strike the package off the
list. Experience and common sense dictate that, in the long run, "bargains"
like that can be very expensive.

Informal Discussions with the Supplier

The first contact with the supplier will probably be with either a salesman,
if the company is large and well established, or for a smaller business, with

one of the principals of the company. This is fine for collecting the initial information for the check lists, but if the project is of major significance it is important to get details directly from one of the designers of the system, preferably an individual who has worked on the project from its inception.

First of all, it is comforting to know that someone who is thoroughly familiar with the system and its history is still associated with it. Secondly, he will be able to answer questions at a level of detail and accuracy that could not be expected from a salesman, however enthusiastic. Finally, he is more likely than a salesman to be objective and able to explain why the package does not have certain features, how easy it would be to make various modifications, and so on.

The meeting with the specialist should not be an aimless chat. Prepare a list of points to ask about in advance, and try to make it as comprehensive as possible to get full value from the meeting and avoid having to go back for answers to questions you forgot to ask the first time. For this reason, this meeting should probably be left until rather late in the project, after the detailed documentation has been studied. If the questions involve system technicalities like file structure and programming techniques, the person to conduct the meeting is obviously the most technically knowledgeable one on the project team, although a representative of data processing management will want to be there as well.

Formal Presentations

Some companies like to ask each of the competing suppliers of a product or service for a formal presentation. This can have a number of advantages:

1. All members of the project team and concerned management can be present and will receive the same information.
2. It offers an opportunity to judge the professionalism and attitudes of the supplier companies.
3. It gives each of the competing suppliers a chance to praise his own product and point out what he thinks are the principal advantages of his system for your company.

If the software selection is part of a larger project for choosing hardware, the formal presentation is almost *de rigeur.*

The prospective user should give each competitor advance warning (at least two weeks) and specify the time limit for the presentation, which could be anywhere from an hour to half a day. Giving plenty of advance notice is not only courteous but also necessary to give the supplier's staff more time to prepare exhibits, diagrams, and data that provide the user with more of the kind of information he wants. Also, the analyst should be sure to give the supplier a fairly detailed outline of what he wants to know and what aspects of the product he is most concerned about: Is it the difficulty of implementation and training, or the design philosophy, or cost? An explicitly stated bid will get the answers.

If possible, the supplier should be informed of the criteria on which the final decision will be made, whether it is value for money, speedy installation, system quality, or whatever, so that he can demonstrate his capability of satisfying the requirements. Systems people who have worked on the system should be present, if they are not actually giving the presentation, as well as salesmen.

In all fairness, each competitor should have the same information beforehand. Some companies who have a reputation for fairness go so far as to allow each competitor to ask questions in advance, and then supply every bidder with a list of all questions asked and the answers. This assures that each one has exactly the same information.

For the sake of recall of all details, as well as the sanity of the project team members, it is wise to schedule not more than two of these presentations on any one day. On the other hand, meetings should be accomplished in fairly rapid succession so that the first one is not completely forgotten by the time the last one is over. This inhibits the possibility of a prematurely positive decision. There is the danger that if the first presentation is very impressive, the judges may be prejudiced in the first competitor's favor and not given an objective hearing to the others, whose efforts may therefore be doomed from the start.

Visits to Other Installations

There may be some value in visiting other installations where a package under consideration is already being used. It would be very unusual to find an identical situation, though, so the differences between the applications and environments should be kept in mind and allowed for. The visits, if they are made, should be considered as a secondary source of information and background.

If other users have not already been identified during the preliminary information gathering, the package supplier should be willing to name some—assuming, of course, that the system has been sold and installed elsewhere—and arrange a meeting with them. It is usually best that the supplier make this initial approach, and try to choose an installation with a similar operation in the same business (if that is not contrary to company policy) or in the same general field. Insurance applications are somewhat similar to those of banks, for example, and many manufacturing operations have the same kind of data processing problems even though the products may be entirely different. Also, if at all possible, the comparison check should be made with a company having the same configuration and operating system.

Be very wary if the supplier says the package is in operation but will not name a user. Only a very small number of companies will refuse to let their names be used in this way. It is unusual to find a data processing manager who is not willing to talk about his systems and give his opinion. If at all possible, go to the installation where the system is running, and talk to both the application users and the data processing people. Ask about both good and bad features as they see them. Even though they may be using a different subset of the system, or different features, their experience in installing and operating the system will be indicative. They will also be able to give information about what to expect from the supplier in the way of cooperation, expertise, and response to questions and problems. It might also be possible to get time-per-volume figures that can be applied to other applications for obtaining time estimates for file creation and system operation.

An often overlooked source of information is a user who has considered the package and then rejected it, or one who used it and has discontinued it. His comments can be very revealing and are likely to be more objective than might be thought. They may be difficult to find, however; unless he is very confident, the supplier will be understandably reluctant to discuss lost sales. A user of one of the possibles on the list, however, might well have considered others the company is interested in, so if he is contacted, inquire about them too. Short of serendipity, the only other way to find these nonusers would be to advertise in a data processing magazine.

Demonstrations

If the software is such that it can be easily demonstrated, the supplier will probably be not only willing but also anxious to do so. The more the demonstration is like a live run, the more valuable it will be. Remember, however, that the more control the supplier has over the demonstration—if he sets it up and has his own people operate it—the easier it is for him to show the best features of the software and gloss over the worst ones.

Use live data if possible, or if not, prepare test data in the installation. The supplier may have his own set of prepared test data, which could save the cost of preparing it, but if the demonstration is worth holding at all it is worth working up at least a few test cases independently. Similarly, use the installation's own hardware—or, if that is not possible, an identical configuration and the same version of the operating system—and the installation's operators, making allowance for the fact that they would be more efficient if they were more familiar with the system. The demonstration might be a benchmark as well, as discussed in Chapter 7. Finally, if a demonstration is held, a presentation will probably be also necessary to allow the supplier to cover aspects of the software not obvious from the demonstration.

WHAT TO FIND OUT

The detailed information collected will vary somewhat, depending on the type of software under study. However, most items will fall under these headings:

The Supplier (and the developer, if they are not the same).
Package History.
Major Trade-offs.
Package Features (file creation, input, updating, processing, retrieval, and reporting).
Operation.
Documentation (system, program, operating, user, and data preparation).
Training.
Contract Terms.

Some of these headings may be irrelevant for some packages. For example, a generalized sort will not deal with file creation as such; detailed program documentation is often not supplied if the software is proprietary and will always be maintained by the supplier; a small utility will have minimal or nonexistent user and data prep instructions and no important training requirements. Recommendations for what information to gather under each of the above headings are discussed in the following sections with some examples. A summary check list is given in Figure 20. This can be used as a guideline for developing a tailored question list for a specific project.

Evaluating the Supplier

The time and effort spent on evaluating the supplier should be directly proportional to both the investment in software and the degree of dependence on the supplier for maintenance. Complete confidence in the supplier's ability and stability is needed if the software is a large package for which programming details will not be revealed. On the other hand, if it is a small programmer aid that is to be maintained by the installation after an outright purchase, it matters very little whether the seller is a corporate giant or a fly-by-night one-man outfit (assuming, of course, that other parts of the evaluation have shown that the program works).

The recommendations in this section for checking out the supplier cover the whole spectrum; they could be abridged for a project of lesser importance. Figure 11 summarizes in check-list format the major points to look for. There are four principal sources for answers to questions about the supplier. The first comprises direct questions to the salesman about principles of the company, which could be verbal or in a formal questionnaire to save time and ensure consistency. This information can be expanded and verified through a credit check, with which the accounting department or the company auditors can help; by studying the supplier's financial reports, if they are available publicly; and through his other clients. The last is possible even if there are as yet no other purchasers of the software in question. If that is the case, ask for the names of other types of clients who have bought other software or other services of the company. Failing this, which can only mean that the company

---

1. Reputation and business integrity
   Business areas
   Age of company
   Clients

2. Size of the company
   Number of employees
   Number of sites
   Expansion plans

3. Financial soundness
   Capitalization
   Profitability

4. Methods of working
   Standards used
   Project-control techniques used
   Staff assignments

5. Expertise
   Background of managers
   Technical ability of systems and programming staff

FIGURE 11: A SUMMARY CHECK LIST FOR EVALUATING THE SUPPLIER

is brand new, business references of the principals can be followed up, i.e., a check with previous employers of the officers.

The general reputation and business integrity of the supplier should head the list of queries. Discussions with one or more of his other clients can bring out whether he conducts himself in a professional manner, is prompt in supplying requested information, meets schedules without fuss, and generally keeps promises. Would clients do business with this company again if the occasion arose? Low turnover and high morale among staff are good signs, too. Behavior in a crisis is indicative as well; check with another client about whether any disasters that occurred could not have been avoided and if the supplier handled the situation in a calm and well-organized manner to get it straightened out as quickly as possible. How highly does the company regard its reputation? Would it forgo a potential quick profit to keep a client happy in the long run? Does it seem to be the kind of company that would advise you *not* to use their services if they honestly felt it would not be in your best interest to do so? Does the staff take pride in its work and the company that employs it? There is no objective test to supply some of these answers, and certain points must be kept in mind throughout negotiations so that periodic appraisal can be made.

If the supplier is relatively unknown, find out what area of business the company is engaged in, and what specialties it has. How long has the company been in business? Check on the numbers of technical (as opposed to managerial, sales, and clerical) staff. If the company has more than one office or site, find out which one is considered to be corporate headquarters; in a business recession or downswing in the company's prospects, the newer and more distant sites are the ones most likely to be cut back or closed down. Would this affect the service you could expect to get? On the other hand, what are their expansion plans, if any? Recent history has shown that small-to-medium companies that attempted to expand too fast were among those who could not ride out the economic recession. A modest rate of expansion, however, indicates that the company is profitable and that its backers are confident.

One should think twice before arbitrarily shunning a small or very young outfit. The experience and reputations of key individuals can supply as much assurance as a well-known corporate name. Moreover, a new company may well give better service—because it is anxious for new business and future recommendations to others—than a giant to whom a single sale more or less does not mean life or death or the difference between a good year and a bad one. Some of the keenest technical people in the data processing business are very unhappy working for a big organization and prefer to go it alone or with a small company. Some very high quality software has been turned out by small companies that do not want to get big, preferring to stay as they are and make a reasonable profit, thus avoiding many of the headaches in a large business structure. If they can measure up to other criteria for integrity and expertise, their size should not be a deciding factor.

Regardless of size, however, a financial check is advisable if the user must rely on their continuance in business to support the software. If possible, check the capital structure of the company: How is it financed and who are the backers? If it is not a public company, who are the shareholders? Is there employee participation, i.e., profit sharing? If possible, check on profitability and credit rating.

The methods of working in the supplier company can be important if contact with them is likely to be a long one, and if a user must rely on them to produce modifications, and supply maintenance, training, and so on, in connection with the software. The supplier should have formal methods and documentation standards; performance standards would be a plus, too. What project control techniques does he use? Formal, upward progress reporting should occur at frequent intervals, especially if the staff is working on a customer's site. Schedules and timetables produced by the finger-in-the-wind method are unreliable; a supplier should be using some objective method of time estimating. If the user will have to rely on him for debugging and emergency maintenance services, it would be reasonable to ask to see his documented procedures for accomplishing this. How will it be decided who is to be assigned to the user's project?

As mentioned previously, expertise of the staff is critical, both managerial and technical. The data processing industry is notorious for the poor quality of its management, which is due partly to the "ex-technician syndrome" whereby the best programmers are promoted to systems work, where they may or may not do as well, and whereby the best systems analysts become managers, a job requiring an entirely different set of abilities and skills. Being able to debug quickly or design an elegant computer system is not an apprenticeship for being able to manage a team and bring a project in on time. If the success of the purchased software depends on managerial skills of the supplier, find out what management experience and success he has had in the past.

The quality of the software is directly related to the expertise of those who designed and wrote it. Check on their previous technical experience and the number of years spent on like work. This should be extended to the application area itself, if relevant; previous design experience carries less weight if the designer knows nothing about inventory control or accounting, or whatever the application area is. What are their credentials for carrying out this kind of work? Is the principal designer still employed by the supplier? Who will be assigned to maintain the purchase? If the user is not the only buyer, the supplier cannot reasonably guarantee to every single customer that the original team will be assigned. Will new people be brought in and trained? If so, how and by whom? Will the buyer have the option of refusing anyone assigned to his installation? If this subject is very important, it may be necessary to get contractual guarantees, discussed in Chapter 9.

If a software broker is not the original developer, it may be necessary to check on the technical expertise of the developer as well. It is especially important in this case to find out who will be supplying support service, what their experience and training with the package is, and what safeguards and guarantees they offer.

Finally, a word about the manner of carrying out this phase of the investigation: It can only be to the buyer's advantage to let the supplier know exactly what is being done and why. Much of the information can come directly from him. The supplier should have no objection to this kind of investigation, and there is no benefit from trying to do it in secrecy.

PACKAGE HISTORY

A few essential questions should be asked about the history of any software offered. It is important to know who originally developed it. If the developer was a single individual, who is he and where is he now? If he is not available for information gathering now, and for modifications or maintenance later, it will be necessary to investigate further the training and qualifications of his successors. The same questions need to be asked if the company selling the system did not develop it. In either case, and particularly when negotiating with a small, new company or an individual, the investigator should establish to complete satisfaction that those offering it for sale really do own it and have a legal and ethical right to sell it. ("Ethical" because of the current muddled situation with regard to software copyrights, discussed in more detail in Chapter 9.)

It is also important to know the age of the package, the history of its development and modifications, and how many have been sold. Some analysts say that "older is better," but that is not necessarily so. Consider the state of the installation's older systems; after several years of modifications, usually by a number of different individuals, systems are apt to become fat and sloppy, held together with chewing gum and string. (A senior analyst at a large insurance company recently commented matter-of-factly that the installation's oldest working system had so many changes in it that "I know there are large blocks of code that are never executed, but I'm afraid to take them out because I don't know what will happen if I do.") On the other hand, a new system has not been proved in actual use. The age of the software has to be judged in to the other evaluation factors, such as its efficiency and the expertise who wrote it and have maintained it.

If the investment in the software warrants, its history may be investigated at greater depth. Inquiries into why it is being offered for sale (other than the obvious reason of profit) may turn up some interesting information. A well-known service company, for example, developed and markets a computer-scheduling system, although its primary business is not software but training and management consultancy. One of its primary motivations was that the company taught and advised certain methods for computer room scheduling and control, and management thought that these should be backed up by a package embodying the principles advocated. In this case, a potential purchaser who had become familiar with those principles by attending one of the company's courses (at a cost that is a tiny fraction of the software cost) would have a good idea of the design philosophy behind the software.

Many programmer aids and utility packages on the market are the result of a strongly felt need, and were developed expressly to meet it. On the other hand, others fall into the category of things you didn't know you needed until you saw them—the result of someone's bright idea to (hopefully) make life easier. An applications package designed specifically to sell will have a certain degree of generalization built in, possibly making it bigger and less efficient than a good hand-tailored system; a package that was originally a user's own system might suit better, but it would have to be a lucky hit if the originator's processing needs exactly corresponded to your own. Adding generalization "after the fact" is difficult to do well if it is to be economical. On the other hand, such a package might be cheaper because the user may not want to make a profit, but just recover its development costs. So, there are things to be said for each type and there are no hard and fast rules. It is best to investigate and evaluate the situation in light of a user's particular requirements.

Not long ago Larry Welke (of International Computer Programs) discovered a payroll package being offered by four different companies and an unemployed unnamed individual. It was the same package in all cases, but the price varied by more than 10 percent, with a variety of support services (57). In such a case, it could pay to ask whether the supplier selected has sole marketing rights to the package.

As a final suggestion for investigation of package history, check its price changes; this may be very interesting. It is rare for a price to be lowered, but if it is, this usually means that the package has been very successful. More often, there will be a history of price increases, sometimes several jumps just between the time the package was announced and its first delivery. It could be that it had been underpriced in the first place, but it is more likely that the developers found it more costly to produce than they first thought (few of us are in a position to cast the first stone here), or that installation assist-

ance to users was greater than anticipated. Sometimes, too, the price is
raised as the first wave of optimism wears off and the sales people find
is not such a huge need for the package as they thought; but there is a point
of diminishing returns on that. Reading between the lines to a salesman's
reply to a question about price increases can give a clue to previous difficulties
with the package, which might then be followed up by a visit to a user.

MAJOR TRADE-OFFS

Trade-offs are important parameters of each package. Most if not all such
compromises will be discovered in the first round of investigation. Seven of
the more usual ones are discussed below.

Price. Because of the variety of ways in which software can be paid for, it
will probably be necessary to convert the prices to some common base. For
example, if the expected life of the system is five years, a straight monthly
rental has to be multiplied by 60 to make it comparative to an outright purchase price, or the purchase price has to be divided by 60. If there is a sliding
scale of rental (say, succeeding years are cheaper than the first), the arithmetic gets a bit more complicated, as it does when maintenance and training
are included in one price but not in another. Moreover, discounted cash flow
and other accounting considerations are factors in a lease versus purchase comparison. The percentages used depend on the company's practices and the
current state of the economy, so it is best to ask the company accountants
for help if in doubt.

Time Required to Implement. Time is especially important if fast installation is high on the criteria list. If it is critical, the supplier's estimate should
be backed with either a proven history (verified on visits to other users) or a
contractual guarantee.

File Sizes. File sizes are expressed in terms of reels of tape, cylinders of disk,
or whatever gives a realistic comparison. Ask the supplier for the base figures,
which may be expressed as a minimum plus the number of records plus a percentage for overhead, and then do your own calculations. Again, these can be
compared to other users' experiences; if the figures collected are in terms of a
ratio of prime data characters to file space, they can be applied to both current and future data volumes. This is especially important for a large, generalized file processor or data management system, for many of these file structures are complex and require a large percentage of available space for over-

head in addition to prime data. If that is not taken into consideration, initial file creation may cause a nasty shock.

Running Time. Again, running time is usually best expressed to a common base such as time needed per thousand input transactions or paychecks, or print lines produced per minute. For multiprogram systems, it may be necessary to calculate the running time of each program and then add them together for total running time per day, week, month. It is usually acceptable to disregard possible savings from running the software under multiprogramming, for if the packages being evaluated do roughly the same things, the gross figures are sufficient for comparison purposes. If running time is critical and is a make-or-break factor in the final decision, technical evaluation will give more refined figures (see Chapter 7).

Configuration and Memory Requirements. These requirements are pretty straightforward, but if operating in a multiprogramming mode is a consideration, the stated configuration (i.e., the supplier's "minimum configuration required") should be refined into requirements for each program.

Operating System Required. Type and version or level of the operating system are checkpoints here. If the installation has not implemented all features of the operating system supplied by the manufacturer, check to see that all those required by the package are operative. Some software may need a special interface with the operating system; any problems this might cause should be investigated.

Source Language. Language may not be particularly important if all maintenance is to be done by the supplier; if not, it will be very important. And if the language is a weird one, as sometimes happens, is the supplier sure of being able to maintain his own expertise in it?

PACKAGE FEATURES

This phase of the study warrants expenditure of the most time and effort. The features of each "possible" must be determined and compared to the specifications laid down in the original study and in the criteria check list previously developed. The basic question to be answered is: Which package comes closest to doing what you want done in the way you want it done? And, is the one that comes the closest close enough?

It is not possible here to give a complete list of questions for each type of software. The check lists can be used to develop specific, tailored lists for each situation. They are expansions of the lists given in Chapter 6 for the feature comparison that produced the short list. If those lists have been compiled, this closer look at the package features can proceed from that point. This detailed study will cover one or more of the following areas: file creation, input, updating, processing, retrieval, and reporting. Not all will be applicable to all types of software. Retrieval is defined as the processing of ad hoc inquiries, resulting in a single item of information or a very small quantity of output, whether in a batch mode or real time; or as opposed to reporting, which is production of prespecified, high-volume reports on a regular cycle, usually in a batch mode. Many systems will have either batch or real-time mode, although some have both. Utility routines, programmer aids, and the like will have no file creation or updating requirements to speak of.

Figures 12 through 17 give the check lists for each of the areas listed above. They are not intended to be comprehensive, but they do cover the more important points under each heading.

---

1. Is the file structure fixed or optional?
2. If optional, who specifies it, the data processing department or the user?
3. How is it specified?
4. Can the files be restructured; if so, how?
5. What physical media are used for the master files? Are there options?
6. How are file names and descriptions specified?
7. How are data descriptions specified and stored? How much space do they take?
8. What are the procedures for file backup? Security?
9. For each file and record format, is there provision for all necessary data?
10. Are the files expansible and flexible enough to handle:
    Processing modifications requiring new data?
    Increases in data volumes?
    Increases in file size?
    Changes in the hit rate?
11. What information is contained in header and trailer labels?
12. How long will initial file creation take?

FIGURE 12: A CHECK LIST FOR DETAILED EVALUATION
OF FILE CREATION FEATURES

1. Will new source documents be required, and if so, what are they and what do they look like? What quantities will be needed?
2. Are the forms easy to fill in? Easy to key from, quickly and accurately?
3. What is the input media (punch cards, paper tape, etc.) and are there any options?
4. Who specifies the input and how?
5. What are the expected volumes per day/week/month? Related keypunch and input reading times?
6. What editing and validity checks are there?
7. What controls are there (batch checks, check digits, hash totals) and how do they work?
8. What error reports are there on input and what do they look like? What is the expected input error rate? Read failure rate (especially for *OCR*)?
9. Who corrects input errors? How long will it take?
10. What controls are there to prevent correctly formatted but fraudulent data from entering the system? (This is especially important for accounting systems.)
11. Will any new input preparation equipment be required? If so, how much will it cost? Delivery times?
12. Will new staff be required for either document preparation or punching? How many?
13. How much user training will be required for preparing source documents? For keypunch staff?

FIGURE 13: A CHECK LIST FOR DETAILED EVALUATION
OF INPUT FEATURES

In addition to the points listed, a separate check list should be prepared for applications packages, covering specific processing related to the application area. For example, if the system is for inventory control, what techniques are used? Do they fit in with existing procedures and the company policy and philosophy? Or, for accounting systems, what accounting techniques are used? Will allowance be made for state and local tax laws? What about billing and payment conventions? For personnel and payroll systems, what about union requirements? It is best to consult with the user (if that has not already been done) before drawing up this check list.

Along with establishing which features each package contains, the analyst must be sure to double-check on whether they are all implemented. If the supplier has stated that the system is already installed and operating in other installations, check to see that all features you are interested in are actually working there.

---

1. What are the file structures and related access methods?
2. Who specifies updating parameters and how?
3. How much flexibility is there?
4. What are the default options?
5. Are error reports produced from updating runs? If so, what checks are included? What do the reports look like?
6. Who will be responsible for error correction? How long will it take?
7. What are the expected updating times for each file per day/week/ month?
8. What happens if there is an abort during updating? What are the re-covery procedures? Specific questions need to be asked depending on the file structure; for example, if chains are used, how can they be repaired if broken? If the files are indexed sequential, what hap-pens if the overflow area gets filled up during updating?

FIGURE 14: A CHECK LIST FOR DETAILED EVALUATION
OF UPDATING FEATURES

---

1. What are the major processes performed?
2. What programming techniques are used?
3. What calculations are performed? What are the formulas? What data is needed for each?
4. What options are there? How are they specified?
5. What internal accuracy checks are there?
6. Is an audit trail established?
7. Are there compress/decompress and encode/decode features; if so, how do they work?
8. Is it possible to insert special processing routines? How?
9. What safeguards are there to prevent unauthorized routines from being inserted?
10. Might the programs be at any time CPU-bound? To what extent? What processing features would be involved?

FIGURE 15: A CHECK LIST FOR DETAILED EVALUATION
OF PROCESSING FEATURES

1. Who specifies retrieval parameters and how?
2. Can the parameters, once specified, be saved for future use?
3. How is retrieval performed?
4. What are sample response times?
5. Through what media are requirements input?
6. What is the possible level of complexity of a request?
7. What types of requests can be handled?
8. Are retrieval statistics accumulated?
9. What are the error-handling procedures?
10. What happens to requests being processed at the time of a system failure?
11. What file, record, and field security procedures are incorporated?
12. For terminal-based systems, what security checks take place? Is there an automatic cutoff or refusal on large-volume output?

FIGURE 16: A CHECK LIST FOR DETAILED EVALUATION
OF RETRIEVAL FEATURES

1. What reports are produced? What do they look like?
2. What is the reporting frequency/cycling?
3. What options are there and how are they specified?
4. What are the default options?
5. What are the report data sequences?
6. How many levels of subtotaling are provided for?
7. Are the reports clear and easy to use?
8. How up-to-date is the information in each report?
9. Do reports provide the information the user needs *when* he needs it?
10. What codes are used in the reports? How will they affect users?
11. What are the expected print times per day/week/month?
12. Will special output forms be needed; if so, what are they and in what quantity will they be available?

FIGURE 17: A CHECK LIST FOR DETAILED EVALUATION
OF REPORTING FEATURES

OPERATION

In addition to the basic operating characteristics set out in the feature check lists, additional and more detailed information may be desirable for the in-depth study. This data falls into two areas, one related to the hardware and internal operating features and the other to the ease of use from the human point of view, both operator and user.

The supplier has probably stated the minimum configuration required in his sales literature, but more details are needed. The minimal requirements, on the one hand, may not be the optimal ones; perhaps the system will run faster on a larger configuration, or with additional peripheral devices. On the other hand, the minimum features may be for the largest program, with smaller ones requiring less. The possible impact on the computer room schedule is obvious, so these things should be determined. If multiprogramming is a con-sideration, core size and central processing unit versus peripheral dominance for each program in the system should be established, as well as the details of modules and overlays that may be called in.

There are special considerations for real-time systems, particularly in the area of response times and CPU dominance. "Average" figures from the sup-plier are not good enough; peak demand rates based on the company's own estimates, given the number of users, number of terminals, and so on, will have to be worked out. Remember that demand will be higher when the sys-tem is first installed, due to the novelty and high error rates.

Under the subject of human convenience, the operating instructions should be reviewed by the operations department. The manager and the computer operators themselves are in the best position to judge how easy or difficult setup, operation, and takedown will be. This depends to some extent on the quality of the documentation, which will be discussed in the next section.

Finally, the error cycle(s) should be reviewed. What will be the elapsed time from detection to correction? Whose responsibility will it be? Is it critical to the processing time of the system, as in some financial applications where all input errors must be corrected before processing can continue? And how are the corrections accomplished?

DOCUMENTATION

The documentation supplied should cover the system, operations, users, and also data preparation and programming, if the software is to be maintained in house. (Training manuals are discussed later.) Some suppliers are understand-ably reluctant to hand over such detailed descriptions of a proprietary package when no commitment has been made, but at the least they should let the purchaser examine samples, if only in their presence. Others are not so distrustful and will allow longer inspection. Do not make any kind of a copy if the material is covered by copyright, as it probably will be. If in doubt, ask.

There are three points on which to judge documentation: completeness, quality, and ease of use. For the first—completeness—one way might be to check it against the installation's own documentation standards for a similar type of system. Figure 18 is a check list for what the documentation should contain by type, if no comparable system is available.

The quality and ease of use is best evaluated by the people directly concerned: the data prep portions by the punch room supervisor, and the program part by a programmer who might be assigned to maintain the system, and so on. Each person will be required to submit a brief evaluative report.

Documentation is not judged solely on a measure of weight or number of pages. A small package such as a utility may need only a few pages in each

SYSTEMS	PROGRAMMING (for each program)
Abstract or summary	Narrative description
Package history	File, input, and output specifications
Outline flowchart	Processing description, with detailed flowchart and/or decision tables
Equipment configuration	Details of special programming techniques used
Operating system and language	Details of subroutines called in
File specifications	Run timings
Input and output specifications	Tables of codes used, switches, etc.,
Data editing and vetting procedures and security	Test plan and sample test cases
Control procedures	I/O samples
Sample timings	Sample console log
Optional: system test description, including test cases	Control card layouts
Glossary or definition of terms	Source listing, label cross-reference list, load map
	Optional: core dump

FIGURE 18: A CHECK LIST FOR EVALUATION OF DOCUMENTATION CONTENTS.

OPERATING DOCUMENTATION

1. Computer (for each program):
   Program name and identification
   Description of program functions
   Summary of peripheral and core
      storage usage
   *Priority and partition, for multi-
      programming
   Estimated running time, by unit
      volume measure
   Inputs, by name and peripheral
      type
   Outputs, by name, peripheral
      type, preparation instructions
   Initial switch settings (if any)
   Description of normal course
      of run
   Samples of all error messages and
      related actions
   Actions in case of program or
      hardware failure
   Restart procedures
2. Data Control:
   *Data reception schedules
   Source document specimens
   Criteria for valid and invalid data
   Procedures for coding source
      documents (if required)
   *Batch and control total procedures
   Input and output quality control
      checks
   *Disposition of source documents,
      input, and output
   Output descriptions
   *Output preparation and labeling
      procedures
   *Take-down instructions, including
      visual labeling and disposal

USER DOCUMENTATION

1. Clerical:
   System description
   Sample source documents
   Source document preparation
      procedures
   Code tables, if any
   Any special procedures, if not
      handled by data control
2. Management:
   System description
   Samples of management
      reports
   Description of each report,
      including intended use
   Code tables, if necessary
   System time cycles

DATA PREP DOCUMENTATION

   Layouts of punching docu-
      ments and media, annotated
   Content of media by field
   *Batch and labeling procedures
   *Error correction procedures
   *Disposal of documents and
      completed media
   *Volume estimates

Note: The asterisk indicates that
content may have to be supplied
by purchaser.

FIGURE 18 (continued)

94

category. Also, some software is overdocumented; that is, documents are overly wordy. Some manufacturer's manuals on programming languages and operating systems are prime examples of verbosity—the same thing could be said in fewer words much more clearly, and better organization would make any particular item much easier to find. These publications suffer the same syndrome as the writer who apologized for sending 3000 words because he didn't have time to write 300.

TRAINING

The evaluation of training must contain answers to four questions:

Who will need to be trained?
How much will be required? (Usually expressed in man-days or man-hours.)
Who will do it?
When should it be done?

The last item is dependent on the delivery schedule and cannot be worked out in detail until the package has been chosen and a delivery date is set. Some indication will be given, however, by the answers to the other three questions.

For a very small package, particularly one to be used only within the data processing department, the training needed will be minimal and might be accomplished entirely through the documentation provided. For a larger system, and especially for an applications package affecting user procedures, training may be a significant item in the budget and in the schedule. When an in-house system is developed, a certain amount of informal training is gained both by users and the data processing staff as the system is specified and tested. This will not be the case when a package is used, so this must be taken into account.

Once the package features are known, a list of potential trainees should be drawn up for each of the departments affected, including systems and programming, operations, user clerical staff, and management. Then, for each group, content and duration of each subject must be listed. In some cases, this will depend partly on the trainees' previous experience; user clerical people, for example, may not have had any previous computer experience and will therefore need introductory education in computer techniques generally before they can go on to the details of the system. A check list of the training content for each group is set out in Figure 19. Once these preliminaries have been outlined, then determine from each supplier:

What training is included in the cost of the package.
Whether extra is available and how much it would cost.
How much flexibility in scheduling is permitted.
Number and qualifications of the staff that will conduct the training sessions.
Staff recommendations for time required and scheduling.
Whether follow-up training will be available for personnel hired after the
 installation of the package.

To verify the supplier's estimates of the amount of time needed for each
group, and to check on the quality, make inquiries when visiting another user.

The amount of training and the instruction capability of the supplier's staff
will be a direct comparison factor in judging each package. For working out
costs (covered in detail in Chapter 8), the time away from the job for each
trainee must be taken into consideration, as well as the time of the in-house
staff conducting the sessions.

SYSTEMS AND PROGRAMMING
    Depends on amount of mainten-
    ance to be done in house, but
    could include:
        General orientation to system
        Interface with operating system
            and other software or other
            systems
        New programming language
        File creation procedures
OPERATIONS
    General orientation to system
    Operation of any new equipment
    System operation
    Control, backup, and security
        procedures
    Handling and dispersal of output
    Operating schedule
    Data control procedures

CLERICAL
    General orientation to system
    Codes
    Data collection and coding
    Input document preparation
    Operating schedule
    Control and recovery pro-
        cedures
    Operation of any new equip-
        ment (e.g., terminals)
MANAGEMENT
    General system orientation
    Report formats and codes
    Data retention and cycling
        procedures
    Audit, control, and security
        procedures
    Operation of any new equip-
        ment (e.g., terminals)
    Formatting retrieval requests
        and interpreting output

FIGURE 19: A CHECK LIST FOR A TRAINING PROGRAM

If the supplier offers training manuals as part of the package, the same general comments as made for other documentation apply. The manuals should be very clear and easy to use; liberal use of illustrations and examples is important, especially for such things as filling in forms and correcting errors.

CONTRACT TERMS

In addition to the cost and other items mentioned previously under "Major Trade-Offs," other details about the contract are needed at this stage. First of all, is a formal contract at all necessary? For smallish packages, a simple purchase order or letter of intent may be all that is called for. On the other hand, if a large amount of money is involved the payment schedule should be set out in a contract. All the extras for training, maintenance, and modification must be determined for the cost/benefit analysis (Chapter 8). The supplier should also mention any unusual or restrictive terms at this time. If possible, a copy of the contract should be reviewed by the company's legal department.

A great many items must be considered in relation to the contract; Chapter 9 is devoted entirely to this subject. For the purposes of the evaluation study, the most important items are the costs. After a decision has been made on a particular package, based on costs and benefits, negotiations can be conducted on the terms, as will be discussed in Chapter 9.

SUMMARY

This chapter has been concerned with in-depth evaluation of the supplier, package features, operation, and documentation of the software and the training that may be required to implement and use it. The summary check list given in Figure 20, however, does not provide all detailed information needed to make a final decision about a major purchase. Subsequent chapters deal with technical evaluation, cost benefit analysis and documenting the results of the evaluation, and contract negotiation.

1. The supplier
   Reputation and business
     integrity
   Size of the company
   Financial soundness
   Methods of working
   Expertise
2. Package history
   Who developed it
   Why was it developed and why
     is it being sold
   Who owns it
   Age and modification history
   Price history
3. Major trade-offs
   Price
   Time required to implement
   File sizes
   Running times
   Configuration and memory
     requirements
   Operating system
   Source language
4. Package features
   File creation, input, updating
   Processing, retrieval, reporting

5. Operation
   Operating environment
   Ease of use
   Error cycles
6. Documentation
   Completeness, quality
   Ease of use for
     systems
     programming
     operations
     users
     data prep
7. Training
   Who is to be trained
   How much time is required
     for each group
   Who is to do it
   When it should be done
   How much is included in
     package cost
   Options and flexibility
   Supplier recommendations
   Follow-up training after
     implementation
   Training manuals
8. The contract
   Terms and payment schedule
   Special provisions or restric-
     tions

FIGURE 20: A SUMMARY CHECK LIST FOR THE IN-DEPTH STUDY

7 | TECHNICAL EVALUATION

Many data processing managers fear that generalized software will be too inefficient for economic operation. Inefficiency is one of the reasons most frequently given for preferring to develop systems in house rather than buy prewritten software. When a decision is made to look at a generalized package, one of the first questions asked is often about its running time and equipment utilization.

EFFICIENCY RATING

The technical or performance evaluation of a piece of software is the process of measuring its efficiency. Efficiency in this context is often taken to mean running time, but in fact it includes a number of other considerations:

1. Amount of internal memory used.
2. Amount of file space used, especially in terms of prime data area versus overhead.
3. Peripheral assignments and utilization.
4. Internal facilities such as compatibility with and fit into a multiprogramming mix.

But the problem all boils down to: "Does the system run as efficiently as it could, given this processing?"

Any reasonably complicated program, even one written by a top-notch programmer, will at first contain logic bugs. Testing is always necessary to find and eliminate them. During testing, performance bugs may be found as well, such as routines and sections of code containing unnecessary instructions, and processing methods that can be altered to speed up running. Any competent programmer will be on the lookout for these as he tests his program. But the user, the systems analyst, the data processing manager, and often the programmer himself sometimes are more concerned that the program does what it is supposed to do; how elegantly and how quickly it performs are items lower down on the list of priorities. With a tight deadline, just getting the program to work is triumph enough.

There may be very good formal test procedures for detecting and correcting logic bugs, but it is rare to find similar procedures for locating performance bugs. The degree of performance efficiency is left to chance, the programmer's expertise, and how much time he has for tinkering to reduce core and speed up execution. Performance bugs are probably just as frequent and just as serious as logic bugs.

The software purchaser wants to protect himself against performance bugs. There are a number of safeguards against logic bugs, which are discussed in other chapters: a history of successful operation, reports from other users, guarantees from the supplier, and so on. Evaluating operating efficiency is not so easy. For example, another user may report that he is satisfied with the running time, but if he has not done a formal evaluation of the system there is no way of knowing whether performance can be improved. "Satisfactory" does not necessarily mean "optimal." Further, it is possible that serious performance bugs exist in parts of the system the other user does not need or uses infrequently; in another installation with different processing requirements, such bugs could seriously affect operational efficiency.

This chapter presents the various ways in which a technical evaluation can be carried out, and discusses its planning and setup. Finally, points for and against doing such an evaluation are given; as will be seen, the process is not always justified.

WHAT TO LOOK FOR IN TECHNICAL EVALUATION

The factors to be studied depend on the type of software and the testing techniques used, but a general list of test factors might include:

1. Utilization of peripheral devices.
2. Input/output wait time.
3. Supervisor entires, frequency and cause.
4. File structures, especially in terms of hit rate, time taken, and space used.
5. Channel usage.

6. Most often used areas of code, subroutines, and similar operations.
7. Throughput by type of processing versus core used.
8. Average instruction time.
9. Shared-program degradation (when multiprogramming).
10. Length of queues and queue handling.

Because most commercial jobs are inevitably input/output bound, the most fruitful areas for investigation will almost always be file handling, message processing, data structures, and peripheral utilization. If the designer of the programs has taken care to optimize things like data segmentation, blocking factors, buffering, queue handling, and peripheral assignments, it is a hopeful indication of the efficiency of the system as a whole. And in any case, for an I/O bound program the efficiency and elegance of the compute sections of the program may not matter at all. The evaluation of the efficiency of systems that are expected to be compute-bound, on the other hand, should concentrate on internal functions like calculations, processing loops, and overlays. Optimization of peripheral usage will not be a critical factor.

A statement often seen in literature is that there is a direct trade-off between amount of core used and running time. This is not true. Many programmers who learned their trade in the days of the second-generation machines will remember jobs for which the primary restriction was core size, and "fitting it in with a shoehorn" was their most difficult task. They can testify to the fact that recoding to reduce the amount of memory used often resulted in more efficient programs just because fewer instructions were used to do the same processing. (Of course, if memory restrictions are so tight that input and output functions are affected, throughput time can be increased considerably.) Only the novice will fall into the trap of thinking that coding for minimal memory size will automatically mean longer execution time; in some cases the exact opposite has proved to be true. The smaller of two programs doing the same thing may be the faster as well.

Methods of Measurement

Seven principal methods of technical measurement are now in use. They are:

1. Visual inspection.
2. Determination of speed per instruction.
3. Measurement of arithmetic data transfers.
4. Benchmarks.
5. Object code comparisons.
6. Direct monitoring via hardware.
7. Direct monitoring via software.

Some important characteristics of these are summarized in Table 3. Some are best suited for a particular type of software, and each has its advantages and disadvantages. Variations in cost and effort are great, too. These differences are discussed in turn below.

TABLE 3. SUMMARY OF TECHNICAL EVALUATION METHODS

Method	Characteristics			
	Requires Operating System with Test or Live Data	Suitable for Systems Software	Suitable for Applications Package	Suitable for Equipment Studies as Well
Visual inspection	No	Yes	Yes	
Speed per instruction	Yes	Yes	No	Yes
Benchmarks	Yes	Yes	Some	Yes
Object code comparisons	Partially	Yes	Some	Doubtful
Direct monitoring via hardware	Yes	Yes	Yes	Yes
Direct monitoring via software	Yes	Yes	Yes	Yes
Simulation (SCERT)	No	Yes	Yes	Yes

Visual Inspection

Visual inspection consists of a study of the system and possibly the individual programs by experienced technicians to evaluate the software on the basis of how well it is designed and written. It requires, at a minimum, that detailed system specifications be available. If the inspection is to go to the level of coding, source programs themselves along with program documentation will be required. Their availability may in itself present difficulties because many suppliers do not readily reveal details of the software.

Assuming, however, that the supplier is willing to lend programs and documentation for a time, an experienced programmer who is really proficient in the source language should be the one to do the program study. He should examine the key areas of coding such as frequently used routines, macros, and loops, so that he can judge how much expertise went into the coding.

Inspection of the detailed system specifications by an expert systems designer can be useful, also. It is best if he is familiar with the application area, if the software is an applications package, or with the type of software being evaluated. If, for example, the subject of study is compilers, it would be desirable for him to have had previous experience with the *design* of compilers, not just their use. He should pay particular attention to file design (structure and access methods) and data segmentation, if it is an I/O bound system. In general, he will want to determine whether the package designer has taken full advantage of the power of the machine and language.

Visual inspection of the system in operation is sometimes recommended, but it is practically useless as a way of judging operating efficiency. Only the most gross performance bugs would be obvious from casual observation of a system being run with test data. If the supplier were so inexpert and foolish as to allow bugs to remain in the software up to this stage, he would (hopefully) have been eliminated from the competition before now. Ease of use from the operator's point of view can almost always be determined from the operating instructions without the necessity of an actual run. (Demonstrations with a broader purpose than estimation of relative speed, however, can be useful, as discussed in Chapter 6.)

The only advantage of a visual inspection of design and code is that, compared to other methods, it is easy and cheap. Actual operation of the system is not necessary. The disadvantages, however, are very severe. First of all, it is necessary to find people qualified to make such an inspection. If they are not available in house, consultants can be called in, but if they are to do a first-class job the fee will be so large that the money would probably be better spent on another type of technical evaluation. (Unless, of course, the consultants are doing the entire evaluation, which is a different case.) Even if someone with the right technical qualifications can be found, his objectivity would be hard to guarantee. The problem of the "not invented here" syndrome has already been mentioned, but even without resentment from in-house staff about the purchase of software, few expert programmers will concede that they could not have done it better. Every programmer has his own idiosyncracies and favorite coding techniques and is bound to be prejudiced, if only unconsciously, against different ones. The problem is not quite so serious with system analysts, but can still exist. A more serious disadvantage is that even a very objective and expert visual inspection may fail to spot huge performance bugs. One example of this was described by Cantrell and Ellison (16). The software under study was an operating system. The method it used to allocate processor time to each of the programs in a multiprogramming mix seemed to designers and evaluators to be fairly reasonable. A detailed study of the system in actual operation, however, suggested improvements that decreased running time by up to half. The difficulty, as can happen with almost any program, was that the actual conditions existing at the time of execution differed from what was expected. Visual inspection will always be subject to that restriction. Finally, any performance bugs found cannot be quantified— it takes live runs to give actual figures for how efficient or inefficient various competing pieces of software are in relation to each other.

Speed per Instruction

Testing for speed per instruction has limited application in software evaluation, being usually reserved for hardware comparisons in which the efficiency of the software, particularly the operating system, is a factor. The best-known method makes use of the Modified Gibson Business Mix, in which each type of instruction is weighted according to its expected use in an "average" commercial installation. Of every 100 instructions for a business application, the mix assumes existence of the following proportions:

    19 adds
    24 compares
    25 moves
    4 edits
    28 unconditional branches
       Total: 100

Given this proportion, the speed of execution is determined. Purported results on different third-generation computers range from 35,460 instructions per second to 2,900 instructions per second. This measures CPU speed as well as the efficiency of the compiler and the operating system, neither of which can be judged separately—all contribute to the result. It ignores variations in configuration, processing environment, and so on. Because it is deemed of little value with high-level languages, the method seems to be less popular than it was in second-generation days.

Arithmetic versus Data Transfers

Check of arithmetic versus data transfers is a measure of how many instructions can be executed while a certain amount of data is being transferred into main memory. Like the speed/instruction method, it measures a combination of hardware speed and software efficiency, and as such has limited application in the evaluation of software in most commercial installations. The best-known of the tests, especially in England, is the Post Office Work Unit (38).

Benchmarks

Benchmarks are another method originally developed for equipment evaluations, but have more application to software problems than the previous two methods. To do a benchmark requires the establishment of a "typical mix" of jobs, which are run through the software being compared, and timed. A number of other comparisons will result, too; for example, ease of use, ease of operation, input preparation, types of problems to be expected, and (because it will be necessary to work closely with the suppliers in setting up and running the tests) indication of what normal service will be like after the system has been installed. This can be done with operating systems, compilers, generalized file processors, data base management systems, and like systems.

If the results are to be meaningful, the test must be based on a truly typical mix of work. Moreover, the mix cannot be typical of past work, but must successfully predict future work loads and requirements. Given that the average life span of a system is five years, the mix should represent the situation that will exist for the next five years, and the various ways in which it will change.

One of the difficulties encountered in practice is that after expending a great deal of time, effort, and money, the results frequently show that there is no significant difference between the various systems being tested. "Significant" here is important, for it is a statistical concept—a difference of a few minutes on a 2-hour run has to be analyzed statistically, not just as a raw item of data. Counting the planning, execution, and analysis of results, the benchmarking of three or four large items of software will take several months at least.

Steve Shirley (52) said:

> Benchmarks appear a natural part of scientific management, another move away from decision-making based on hunches, feelings, opinions, and all the things we call "experience" but cannot quantify; a move towards decisions based on facts, or if not facts then probabilities. Measure, experiment, assess in quantitative terms, compare and contrast. . . . You can then compare like with like, not oranges with apples. And after you've paid all the bills, you too have done a benchmark.

Her conclusion was that they are rarely worth the expense involved.

Object Code Comparisons

Code comparison is a fairly simple procedure and can be carried out without too much trouble or expense, although its usefulness is somewhat limited, being applicable only to items of software that produce object code from source statement inputs. These would include things like compilers, assemblers, some generalized applications packages, decision table processors and macros,

and some debugging aids. A typical program or unit of code is compiled, and
the compile times, execution times, and size of the blocks of code generated
are compared. For an assembler or compiler, key features can be chosen, such
as frequently used macro sequences.

One company used this method to compare a decision table processor to
hand coding of the same problem. In one test, the decision table program took
slightly more core (9.5K as opposed to 8.5K) and the running times were exactly the same, but debugging time for the decision table version was considerably less. In another test, the decision table processor took only 3.8K, while
the hand-coded program required 4.8K. Running times were again comparable.
The test showed up ways in which use of decision tables could be made easier
for the systems analysts, and also gave rise to some suggestions to the supplier
for improving the software. The company was very pleased with the results
and instituted the use of decision tables and the software package for the entire installation.

The difficulties with this method are that care must be taken to ensure that
the test problem is indeed typical of the situation as it will be in real life; an
atypical test case can produce either falsely good results or falsely bad ones.
In the first instance the true situation may not come to light until it is too
late to change or recoup the investment; in the second, the failure will probably never be known and the installation could have lost out on a good thing.

Direct Monitoring

Monitoring is the newest of the technical evaluation techniques and the one
that holds the most promise for software purchasers. It is applicable to any
type of software. There are a number of different methods, but most analysts
use a sampling technique whereby a program resides in memory with the program under study and samples at intervals what is happening in the problem
program. For example, entries to the supervisor may be monitored to see if
the most frequently used routines are resident.

While it might be possible to write the necessary routines in house, it would
probably be cheaper and certainly quicker to use one of the many services or
products on the market for software monitoring and evaluation. The examples
given below have been chosen for illustrative purposes, and represent only
some of the possibilities. Details of prices and suppliers for the ones mentioned
here and others are given in Appendix B.

Some of the systems use a hardware "black box" to monitor what is happening in the central processor. As implied, one purchases the service rather than
a product. It is attached to the CPU—the only time taken from normal processing is the hookup time. No software is required. The result is a report on

event time versus elapsed time for such things as compute time, system active time, partition busy time, operating system overhead, and software overhead. Or, you can buy your own black box. Most manufacturers will either supply this service or put you in touch with a company that does. This hardware approach was obviously designed for overall evaluation of computer usage. The service is relatively inexpensive, however, and does not require interference with the operation of the software being tested. It would be necessary, as with a benchmark, to construct a typical mix of jobs if the software under study is to perform, with the attendant problems and dangers.

Another version of direct monitoring uses software rather than hardware. One such is Boole and Babbage's Systems Measurement Software/360. The Problem Program Efficiency (PPE) version consists of two programs, an extract that resides in the same partition with the program being evaluated, requiring about 6K, and an analyzer that produces a report on the result, requiring a 24K partition. Among other things, it measures I/O wait time by file, areas of the program most frequently used, and I/O-to-compute ratio.

Another monitoring technique is Lambda Corporation's LEAP. This, again, is a stand-alone program that monitors the problem program and produces graphs and statistics on such things as entries to subroutines, channel usage, queues, and device usage.

One technique which does not require running the software to evaluate it is the Systems and Computers Evaluation and Review Technique (SCERT) from Comress. For readers not familiar with SCERT, the following is a brief general description quoted from the sales literature: "SCERT is an integrated system of close to fifty programs which simulate computer applications on various hardware software configurations, providing objective, detailed projections of the performance to be expected." It is operated as a service, with the Comress staff defining the input parameters. It will do anything from specifying the best computer configuration for a company to setting the optimum multiprogramming mix. On the software side, the programs can be evaluated for operational efficiency, with specific recommendations for how each program could be improved.

Each of these examples and the others mentioned in Appendix B were designed with the goal of optimizing the efficiency of programs; it is assumed that corrections will then be made to the performance bugs thus detected. But they can be, and have been, effectively used to evaluate the performance of a number of software packages to help choose the most efficient one. When this is done, the supplier of the package finally chosen can be asked to improve the system on the basis of the information gained, or such improvement may be a condition for purchase.

SETTING UP AND CONDUCTING THE TECHNICAL EVALUATION

The assignment of personnel to the project team was discussed in Chapter 4. The people who perform the technical portion of the evaluation should be the ones having the most experience with the internal workings of software, and having the most programming proficiency. In some situations, such as the evaluation of an operating system, it is almost mandatory that the individual also have intimate knowledge not only of how such software works, but also of the design philosophy behind it.

The important initial step is to make an overall plan of what will be tested and how it will be done. For benchmarks, as an example, this means dividing the technical evaluation into three phases, planning and working up the test cases, conducting the benchmarks, and then evaluating the results. Each of these phases can be further broken down into smaller steps as necessary. For large packages, the planning is best done by classifying the facilities of the software and devising test procedures for each individually, as well as for the overall system.

For example, the facilities of a full-scale operating system could be classified under the following headings:

File and Data Handling
Job Loading and Scheduling
Queue Handling
Multiprogramming
Compiler Efficiency
Program Libraries
Error-Handling and Recovery Procedures
Security
Utility Routines
Accounting and Operating Statistics

A generalized file processor or data base management system might be divided into file creation, file updating, data manipulation, batched report generation, and on-demand inquiry responses. Such segmentation will not only make the job easier, but will also provide more meaningful results. For example, it is almost always the case that complex data structures needed for very fast retrieval require lengthy updating procedures. The technical evaluation, by providing exact measures of each, will enable the final selection to be made on a comparison of the relative times taken by the various software packages, on the balance between the installation's need for fast retrieval, and on the updating time it can tolerate. It also makes easier the comparison of several different packages, when some features exist in one but not in another.

Implied in the description of the various evaluation methods was the fact that it is usually necessary for members of the project team to have thorough knowledge of the software they are evaluating. First, it will be necessary to set up appropriate test procedures, and then to interpret the results. The only situation for which this might not be true is one where the evaluation was done on a service basis by outsiders; even so, judging their results must ultimately be the task of management or someone on the project team. The time needed for this should be taken into account when planning the project.

In fact, the process of evaluation will in itself be a learning situation for members of the project team. Cantrell and Ellison (16) put it more elegantly:

> All good analysis consists of a combination of theoretical analysis and empirical measurement. This is the classic "scientific method". . . . Neither theory nor measurement alone is sufficient. Theoretical analysis alone may solve a nonexistent or unimportant problem. Measurement alone often misses a few critical parameters needed to test the theory. Since neither can stand alone, analysis usually consists of successive applications of the classical theory/measurement/revised theory/revised measurement/etc., cycle. It is important to recognize the iterative nature of analysis, the theory/measurement cycle. Successive cycles revise or obsolete previous concepts. Therefore, time spent in polishing the first theory or the first measurement method will almost certainly be wasted.

IS TECHNICAL EVALUATION NECESSARY?

Serious consideration should be given before deciding to do a technical evaluation. All methods that could be used, except for visual inspection (which is of doubtful value, as discussed above), require computer time and a considerable amount of advance planning and time spent on evaluating the results. Most methods require what amounts to a live run, whether or not the data used is real or test data. Even after all the effort and expense, the results could (and frequently do) show no significant differences between the systems being tested. Therefore, the exercise must always be regarded as a risk venture.

The most compelling reason for an evaluation of efficiency is expected frequent use of the software requiring relatively high percentages of computer time. For example, a 30-second difference in the running time of a compiler's being used once or twice a day on average would not be important, but if it were used dozens of times during a shift, it might be well worthwhile to see whether faster versions were available. Or, a print utility expected to be used heavily, for all installation print output, should probably be checked to make sure that it is taking best possible advantage of the speed of the printer. In one university computing center with a time-sharing scientific environment, where the average execution time of programs was measured in seconds, several different versions of the link loader (the software that called programs into core) were evaluated, and it was found that the difference between the slowest and the fastest was on the order of several hundred percentage points. As it was used hundreds of times a day, the saving in time was significant when a switch was made to the faster version. But the average applications package, and even most systems software in a commercial installation, is used relatively infrequently. A little arithmetic will prove the point.

Take the example of two programs being evaluated, one requiring 25 minutes a week and the other 30; the difference mounts up to slightly over 4 hours a year. A benchmark, say, will take at least that much in machine time, to say nothing of staff time. On the other hand, if the program were to be run twice a day, the difference would be almost 1 hour a week and 43 hours a year. The difficulty is, as pointed out above, that it cannot be known whether or not there is a difference until the evaluation has been completed. And, of course, the examples assume that there is no other difference between the choices, for both perform the same processing. If the slower program is also the more desirable because of extra features, the results of a technical evaluation will have to be taken in relationship to the other parts of the evaluation.

As the relative costs of machine time decrease and the costs of human (programming and management) time increase, a historical trend that shows some signs of slowing down but will never be reversed, the justification for doing a technical evaluation decreases.

Other reasons for the evaluation include the possibility of giving the staff experience in doing it. This might justify testing a small item that would be used infrequently because a project involving a much larger and more critical system is coming up. On the other side of the coin, a staff that is not expert at doing this type of study, especially if working to a tight deadline, may well produce erroneous or meaningless results. If it is desired to build up the expertise of the programmers and analysts in this area, careful records should be kept of the predicted times (based on the evaluation) versus actual times taken once the system has become operational. An investigation into why differences occurred can be of considerable learning value. Also in favor of an efficiency test is that for a second-generation machine (or if third-generation equipment is heavily loaded and every minute counts) the ratio of computer cost versus staff cost may be different, making the technical evaluation more worthwhile.

There are a number of alternatives to the technical evaluation:

1. Do Nothing. This is often the most economic choice if the decision rests between a single software package and doing the job in house. Any categorical statement that the in-house system would be more efficient would have to be based on objective evidence—that is, an evaluation of the installation's own system (perhaps with one of the monitors mentioned) showing that no improvements are possible. Few installations have done this, and fewer yet have had positive results. If the claims of the suppliers of the monitor are to be believed, the average installation saves from 10 to 50 percent of processing time through the use of their products, which does not speak very well for the initial efficiency of the systems. The undoubted higher expertise of employees of software companies, coupled with their concern to make the software as efficient as possible (it could make or break the success of the product, a consideration few private installations have), will probably at least balance out any efficiency lost because of generalization of the software.

2. Take results obtained by other users of the software if the processing requirements and usage are truly similar.

3. Ask the supplier: Perhaps he has himself done an efficiency evaluation and tune-up before offering the software for sale. Ask to see the results of the tests.

4. Obtain guarantees of running times, based on unit volumes of processing. This is discussed in more detail in Chapter 9, under "Contract Negotiation."

This discussion of pros and cons is summarized in Table 4.

TABLE 4. REASONS FOR AND AGAINST DOING A TECHNICAL EVALUATION

Yes	No
Package is expensive.	Package is inexpensive.
Possibilities are otherwise equal.	One possibility is clearly the best otherwise.
Execution time will be long.	Execution time is short.
Frequency of use will be high.	Software is used infrequently.
Heavily loaded hardware and/or second-generation machine.	Third-generation machine.
Evaluation would be inexpensive.	Evaluation would be expensive.
Other benefits expected from technical evaluation.	No internal expertise available to do it.
	Developer has done technical evaluation.
History of package is doubtful and no guarantees are available.	Other users have done technical evaluation.
	Supplier will give guarantee.

COST/BENEFIT
ANALYSIS

When the evaluative and technical studies have been finished, it is up to the project team to make recommendations, and to data processing and user management to make a choice based on the data presented. The analysis of costs and benefits depends on the information previously collected: data about the software and the suppliers, the results of the technical evaluation, and the original feasibility study or user request presenting the problem and the objectives the new system must meet. The question to be answered now is: What solution best meets the user's needs at a price he is willing to pay?

The choice may be between several different software packages, buying software or doing it in house, or possibly between buying software and doing nothing. The last is especially likely to arise in the case of small-scale software such as a program documentation package or test data generator—i.e., programmer aids and utilities. In that case a full cost/benefit analysis is hardly worthwhile, nor is the preparation of a formal report on the results of the study. If two or more of the possibilities give much the same service, the decision is made simply on the basis of which is the cheapest. Otherwise, the previous study of the features of each will have made clear which one best suits the needs of the installation; then the purchase can be made without further ado.

For a more important system, however, the cost/benefit analysis can be critical. The wrong decision could mean at best, an unnecessarily high expenditure for the system, and at worst, breakdown of the user's procedures, his inability to provide his particular service for the company, and the generation of hostility and distrust between the user departments and data processing. It is the responsibility of the software selection project team to summarize and analyze the respective costs and expected benefits of each of the alternate solutions, to do it accurately, to present the results to the user in a form he can understand, and to make recommendations. The final decision must be the user's, particularly in a situation where he can spend more or less money for more or less service from the computer system.

This chapter presents the principles of doing a cost/benefit analysis, which are the same no matter what the subject matter, but with special emphasis on the problems peculiar to deciding between buying a package or developing an in-house system. Costs are discussed first, with particular attention paid to identifying all the costs associated with buying software. Unhappy results are likely when an understanding of the true cost of buying software is lacking. Second, methods of identifying and weighting benefits are discussed, followed by the subject of balancing costs and benefits to arrive at a wise decision. Various alternatives for different situations are suggested. The final topic is documentation of the results of the study: the evaluation report, with suggestions for its content and format. As in previous chapters, key points are summarized in check lists.

DEVELOPMENT COSTS

In order to make an intelligent decision, all costs associated with each of the alternatives have to be established. The types of errors frequently made in data processing when estimating costs are to neglect itemizing all the costs and to be too optimistic. The first results from inexperience or unfamiliarity with the actual costs of running systems, particularly in the user department. The second often happens when the project team or manager has already made a decision and is now attempting to justify it, or because of failure to take into account inevitable future increases in the cost of staff and supplies.

Costs are of two general types, direct and indirect. Indirect costs may be caused by the effect on user operations when the staff no longer has visible records available because the system has been changed from manual to a computer-based one; another cause may be the increased cost of making changes to a computer system, inevitably a more complex and more expensive procedure than any occurring in the old manual system. These two things, in fact, represent the major and very real disadvantages of computers as opposed to manual paper-work systems. Although it would be theoretically possible to measure these costs, the exercise would be so difficult and time consuming that it is rarely or never done, and almost as rarely taken into account when planning computer systems.

Of direct costs, the major item is almost always staff, clerical and management. Physical resources contribute almost as much. These include equipment (data preparation equipment and off-line machines as well as the computer) and other resources needed for carrying out the system, anything from typewriters to vehicles, as well as overhead support of both staff and equipment.

Money is expensive, too; this is one easily measurable direct cost that is sometimes neglected in developing computer systems. It may take the form of interest, either on money borrowed to finance the system or, more usual, the interest lost because the money cannot be invested elsewhere. Other "money" costs are associated with the computer system itself, such as the form of credit control procedures, altered cash flow, or optimization of ordering to take advantage of discounts, although the benefits obtainable from these are quite likely to increase money value rather than decrease.

If the decision is to make or buy, the costs of developing the system in house will have to be worked out in order to compare them to software costs. The rule here (which applies equally to costing the software option) is to be pessimistic. It is rare to hear about a project that took less time and money than originally estimated, but hardly anyone complains when it does happen. If all the sets of costs worked out are equally conservative, any error on the side of pessimism will be balanced, and a long-term result of praise for the data processing department for doing the job efficiently (no matter which alternative is chosen) is more to be desired than inevitable disillusionment because of overly optimistic estimates.

Working with a past history of project estimates and costs is one of the best ways of arriving at realistic estimates for future projects, but unfortunately few installations keep a history of the original estimates, the revisions, and the final actual costs for comparison purposes. With the exception of a simple, isolated application, circumstances can change so quickly during the time the system is being written that the original estimates become invalid anyway. The solution to the problem is to set up better standards for estimating and controlling systems work. Organization of such standards is beyond the scope of this book. Even if it was not, good standards need to be in operation for a while before they can be validated and full benefits realized.

The major cost items in developing a system in house are outlined in Table 5. Other costs incurred in the data processing department which could affect the final price of the system are:

1. New staff: programmers, analysts, or management.
2. Recruitment costs.
3. Staff training, either special training associated with a particular system or training of recruits.
4. Travel expenses for systems analysts in visiting users, and/or for programmers when testing at a remote site.

These are in addition to the usual overhead costs, of course, but they are the ones most often forgotten.

The major costs of buying software are also listed in Table 5. Additional costs not included in the table might be:

TABLE 5. COSTS OF IN-HOUSE DEVELOPMENT VERSUS SOFTWARE

Category	Percent of total cost	
	In-House	Software
Application selection, user request, feasibility study	7–15	7–15
Software evaluation	–	7–20
Software purchase price	–	30–40
Data gathering and analysis	8–22	4–11
System design	5–15	–
Programming	25–35	–
System testing	3– 7	–
File conversion	10–15	10–15
System installation	7–10	9–13
Documentation	6–10	2– 4
Training	2– 5	4– 6

1. Specifications and correspondence with suppliers.

2. Visits to suppliers.

3. Visits to other users.

4. Any travel connected with the evaluation.

5. Reference materials (e.g., books, magazines, software services).

6. Consultants' fees.

7. Extra machine time for the technical evaluation and/or the acceptance test, if more than one package is tested.

8. Legal fees connected with contract negotiation, or the time of the company lawyer or legal department.

9. Optional extras of the package.

10. Accommodation and facilities for the supplier's staff while installing the package or training company staff.

Neglect of these "extras" when doing the original estimates can lead to a nasty shock later on.

Table 5 also includes relative percentages of the total cost that could be reasonably expected to be spent on an in-house system, as opposed to software. These are fairly rough figures, based on the experiences of many companies. The relative percentages would be the same in most parts of the industrialized world, although the total cost may be lower in countries like England where salaries and other costs are generally less than in the United

States. Special circumstances, though, could alter these percentages dramatically. For example, one company as a matter of policy does a detailed system design before investigating software in order to compare its approach to that of packages, altering the proportions spent on design versus the final purchase price of the software.

The cost of the initiation of the project will be about the same, but (as pointed out earlier) it is usually necessary to do a feasibility study before software is even considered as an alternative. The cost of the evaluation will vary, depending on how many possibilities are investigated and on whether a technical evaluation was done, but if it goes much higher than 20 percent of the total cost (unless there are unusual circumstances), the whole value of the exercise could be questioned.

The range of 30 to 40 percent of the total as the purchase price of the package is conservative. Companies with staff of higher than average expertise, especially those with previous experience in selecting software, could expect this to be closer to 50 percent. Some companies who have a very careful evaluation procedure, however, estimate that the total cost will average three times that of the purchase price, with only marginal improvements possible.

The next steps disclose the areas where the savings associated with software show up. The costs of data gathering and analysis will not disappear altogether, however, especially for an applications package. The major portion of these will be for designing the input subsystem procedures and forms, with a smaller portion necessary if there are options in the output. Systems design and programming, which when taken together can add up to half the cost of an in-house system, do not exist for software. The exception to this would be if in-house modifications were made to the package. Similarly, software will probably not require systems testing for debugging purposes. The costs of the acceptance test are included in system installation, which is why that percentage is higher than for an in-house system. File conversion costs are about the same.

A small percentage is allowed for documentation of software because it may be necessary to write all or some of the manuals in house if those supplied are not adequate, do not conform to company standards, or do not meet special requirements. In any case, it is probably advisable to have extra copies made.

Training represents a smaller proportion of cost for a system developed in house solely because a certain amount of informal training is inevitable while the system is being designed and written, which would not occur if the system were bought. This fact must also be kept in mind when preparing the training schedule.

USER'S COSTS

The user department's costs must be taken into consideration in the total cost of the system. Exactly what these are will depend on the standard practices of the company, but they usually fall into five areas, as described below.

Feasibility study. This accounts for anything from the time spent by people being interviewed to a full-time liaison assigned to the project team. These costs may be reflected in overtime.

File conversion. Conversion time is costly, especially if the computer files are being built from manual records. Checking the new files and inserting corrections can be a user's nightmare. Costs may involve overtime, temporary staff, duplicating records that cannot be spared long enough for keypunching, and possibly the indirect cost of loss of profits due to the staff's being unavailable for its usual work.

System implementation. The user's help may well be required during system testing, and certainly will be during the first few cycles of a new system. Parallel running may double or treble the amount of work the department must do. Assuming that the machine time is not being charged to the user, major items will be overtime and wages for temporary employees.

Elimination of staff. In the unlikely event that the new system will actually reduce the number of employees needed, there will be the costs of retirement payments, notice pay, or retraining of staff. An indirect cost, very difficult to measure, could result from low morale and resistance to the new system. Special bonuses may have to be paid to keep staff until they are no longer needed.

External liaison. The cost of indoctrination of customers, or suppliers, or general public relations must also be considered if the system will have any effect on external activities.

OPERATING COSTS

Gathering the development costs is only half the battle. Estimated operating costs must be worked out too. These will have to be based on the life expectancy of the system, which, unless there are very unusual circumstances, will be the same for a system developed in house or a software package. If the package is to be leased, life expectancy could be the term of the lease; otherwise, five, six, or seven years are reasonable figures to use.

The two largest items in the operating budget will be data preparation and computer time. Input preparation, in fact, can amount to as much as 50 percent of the total cost of running the system. Figure 21 shows the off-line operating steps of a typical batch system. Associated with each item will be staff costs and overhead, and the costs of equipment and supplies. Remember that all these operations are very likely to cost more in the future than they do today; therefore, an incremental factor must be reflected in each year's total when estimates covering the life of the system are projected.

To determine the costs of computer processing itself, it is first necessary to know the approximate running time of the system. In the case of software,

---

INPUT

Data origination and collection

Clerical checking and validation

Keying (creation of computer media)

Clerical checking of computer media (batch controls, etc.)

COMPUTER PROCESSING

OUTPUT

Decollating

Bursting

Binding

Off-line copying

Binding

Distribution

FIGURE 21: OFF-LINE STEPS IN SYSTEM OPERATION

this should have been determined at an earlier stage in the evaluation (see Part III), and may be later stipulated in contractual arrangements. The installation will probably have its own standard figures for computer time. Determine whether these figures include all overhead, staff costs, supplies, and so on; if not, they will have to be added. Future plans of the installation have to be taken into account, too; purchase of different computer equipment or extension of the present kit could either lower or raise the running cost, depending on the circumstances.

Finally, some of the costs listed under the heading of development will also occur after the system has been implemented. The need for maintenance will be inevitable. In the case of a home-grown system, maintenance may well go through all steps in the original exercise, from feasibility study to system testing and file conversion. The most realistic way to estimate these is to use the history of systems already implemented, and compute relative percentages based on the size and complexity of the new system. For installations without previous experience as a guide, 10 percent of the cost of development per year would be an optimistic estimate; and a conservative one would be 20 percent. Extensive revisions to the system have to be considered as a new development project rather than as maintenance. Determining this figure for the software package will be easy if maintenance is covered either by the purchase or rental price or by a separate agreement. Nevertheless, the installation will probably have to supply machine time for testing changes.

Other extras associated with the on-going cost of running the system could include further documentation and training. Staff turnover, sometimes even before the new system is implemented, creates this need. It may be advisable to conduct periodic refresher courses for existing staff.

BENEFITS OF A COMPUTER SYSTEM

In a business environment, the principal benefits of a computer system over a manual one fall into the general category of improved speed and accuracy. Because of the speed with which processing can be done on a computer, direct savings—or more likely, a curtailment of an otherwise inevitable increase in costs—can be effected in certain staff functions (the jobs being eliminated rather than the people) and in the costs of off-line equipment such as accounting machines. Speed of processing may also increase the profitability of the company, either directly—as when faster invoicing improves the cash flow position or better credit control reduces bad debts—or indirectly through better service to the customer. Accuracy must be linked to speed in this context, for without the former the latter is valueless.

Another category of benefits exists because computers can perform tasks that would otherwise be impossible within a realistic time scale. The most obvious examples are in the scientific area, but even within a commercial environment many companies are now doing things like optimization of transport, inventory control, and modeling, which previously would have been totally uneconomic without a computer. And some companies—the paper mills like banks and insurance companies particularly—could not have expanded as they have without computers to do the repetitive but relatively uncomplicated processing.

It is extremely difficult to measure this type of benefit with any degree of accuracy. Unless someone with experience can be called upon, the usual course is either to call them "intangibles" and base the justification for the system only on the quantifiable benefits, or to classify the whole project as a risk venture analogous to other research and development projects.

For the software selection project, the desired benefits of the new system will have been laid down in the user request or feasibility study. The problems are first determining which benefits each of the alternative systems will supply; second, assigning a value or weight to the benefits, to balance against the cost; and third, deciding which solution gives the highest ratio of benefit to cost, or if the purchase is a simple yes-or-no decision, deciding whether the benefits outweigh the costs. The three phases listed above will be considered here in sequence. The procedure for solving the third problem involves a subset of the full-scale cost/benefit analysis.

Determining the Benefits

If the preliminary work of getting information about each package and setting it out in an orderly format has been done properly, determining the benefits offered by each alternative will be partly a mechanical process. If one or more solutions offer additional benefits not originally projected, some reconsideration is necessary. If such peripheral gains are minor, they will provide some extra attractiveness without significantly influencing the final decision. If they are major, and would tip the scales, perhaps it will be necessary to go back and incorporate them in the feasibility study. It is dangerous to make the final choice solely on the basis of desirable benefits not discovered until a certain software package containing them is found. This event requires careful reconsideration of the whole purpose of the new computer system.

One tactic that might be adopted with success is letting the software supplier specify which requirements his package will meet. This means sending each supplier a copy of the feasibility study, or preparing a special document that includes information about the business environment, problems, and desired benefits. The supplier is then invited to state in his reply what his product will do to supply the benefits, and how the package can accomplish it. The difficulties of this method in practice are that the supplier may not answer directly, preferring to submit a general sales blurb, or that he will not answer in enough detail. With some persistence, however, even the most evasive vendor can be pinned down. Most suppliers will answer fully and honestly, even going so far as to say what their system will not do. It is not to their advantage to misrepresent their products when the facts would become obvious once a system was installed. Nevertheless, if the decision to purchase hinges on the supplier's statement that his system will supply the benefits, this must be made a condition of the contract. This is especially important if, because of the supplier's desire for secrecy to protect his product, his answers do not include details of how the benefit can be achieved. (Contract negotiations are discussed in Chapter 9.)

Weighting Benefits

In the systems analysts' heaven, one and only one solution will meet all requirements—and it will certainly be the cheapest. In real life it is often necessary to make trade-offs. It is therefore helpful to be able to weight each benefit in proportion to its importance in relation to all the others. The most obvious way to do this is to determine the monetary value of each, say, as staff savings: How many employees at what salaries? As equipment savings: What items at what cost? As reduced inventory: How much; what value? The money value becomes the weight of the benefit. This method is ideal, but few business activities can be so easily quantified. For example, what value can be assigned to "better service to customers" or "more timely information," which are two of the intangible benefits commonly offered by computer systems? Any monetary value chosen is a guess; an informed guess, perhaps, but it can never be accurate or reliable enough to qualify even as an estimate.

An alternative method of weighting is ranking. Each anticipated benefit on the list, tangible and intangible, is given a rank, placing it in relative position to the others. The best person to do this is the user. Asking which benefits are the most important is not exact enough; human nature being what it is, most of the items will end up in the "essential" category and no progress will have been made. One way to avoid this is to allot 100 points to be divided between the items. Better yet, ask that the benefits be placed in a list in descending order of desirability, the most important at the top. For tangible benefits to which a monetary value can be attached, the ranking will place those with the biggest saving at the top of the scale. Nevertheless, intangible benefits, or those difficult to appraise monetarily, may rank higher. The procedure can be taken one step further by dividing the items into three groups, those at the top of the list being essential, followed by the middle group of highly desirable ones, and the last group of nice but nonessential features. The subdivisions can be finer if desired, but three are usually enough.

Comparisons of Solutions

When values and weights have been assigned to the desired benefits, and when the development, purchase, and operating costs have been calculated, comparisons of the various solutions under consideration can be done. Three basic approaches for doing this are: formula method, standard costing method, and cost/benefit analysis by feature. In practice, more than one of these methods might be used in the same project, subsequent ones being tried to verify or expand on the results of the first, or any one of a variety of modifications can be introduced, depending on the details of the problem and the ingenuity of the systems analyst. Whatever method is used, it must be acceptable to the user and to the company accountants. The theme throughout this discussion has been that the evaluation must be as systematic and as objective as possible, which is particularly true for the cost/benefit analysis.

Formula Method
The formula method for cost/benefit analysis is straightforward once the appropriate figures have been gathered. The data needed for each alternative solution is:

1. Total cost up to the date of installation. (For software, this means the purchase price plus installation costs; for own-system, development and implementation costs.)
2. Elapsed time to possible installation of the system.
3. Operating costs per time unit.
4. Savings per time unit.
5. Expected life of the system.

The time unit chosen may be days, weeks, months, or years, as long as it is the same for all figures. Weeks or months are usually the best to work with. The expected life of the system, for the purposes of this formula, is assumed to be same for each alternative. After the time unit is selected perform the following calculations for each alternative:

1. Multiply the operating cost by the expected life.
2. Add that to the development/installation cost.
3. Multiply the savings by the expected life.

If savings are less than costs, the system has a negative value; that is, it will cost the company more than it saves. As has been pointed out, that may be acceptable if the intangible benefits outweigh cost considerations.

The calculations should be taken one step further. If the elapsed times to installation are not all the same, take the difference between each one and the longest one. Multiply that by the expected savings and add the result to the savings side of the equation, to take into account the benefit of getting on the air sooner. For example, the results of the first calculations might be:

System A: Net saving of $100,000
System B: Net saving of $90,000
System C: Net saving of $85,000

But system C may be able to run six months sooner than either of the other two. If the expected savings from C are $1000 a month, it is a better investment than B, but still not better than A.

Standard Costing Method

The formula method is easy to apply, once the figures are available, and can give a fast approximation. But, because it ignores a number of important factors, it may not be good enough for a large-scale system where the potential benefit (or loss) to the company could be great. Either as the next step or as an alternative, standard costing methods can be used to compare the proposed solutions.

Only a brief description will be given here. For real-life applications it would be wise to consult staff accountants about the standard practices in use in the company. Or, the procedures used in previous costing/feasibility studies in the installation can be followed. Table 6 shows the basic layout of the cost analysis. Such an analysis should be prepared for each alternative, that is, for software packages and in-house developed systems. Each of the cost and savings headings in Table 6 should be supported by detailed breakdowns. To get the final analysis all on one page, the usual practice is to do these separately and take the totals for the summary, as shown here. Intangible costs and benefits, for which realistic figures are unattainable, should not be included. These can be set out elsewhere as "advantages and disadvantages."

The development/purchase/installation costs cover all those items discussed previously, including the price of the package or the cost of developing the system in house, and all testing and conversion costs. For an in-house system, the last item will be expendable after installation, but for rented software it would be carried across each year of the life of the package.

All costs should be shown in the year in which they will occur. Taking the total development cost of the system and dividing it by the life-span of the

TABLE 6. LAYOUT OF COST ANALYSIS FIGURES

Item	Year 1	Year 2	Year 3	Year 4	Year 5
Development/purchase/ installation costs					
Maintenance					
Operation					
Equipment					
Total costs					
Savings					
Other benefits					
Total savings					
Net balance					
DCF* factor					
Discounted balance					
Cumulative discounted balance					

*Discounted cash flow.

system to spread the cost out is not realistic. If the company will have to spend all of allotted money in year 1, that is where it must be shown. Spreading the one-time development costs over the life of the system might be done by the accountants for tax or other purposes (although even that is becoming less popular); but this should not be done in a cost/benefit analysis.

Continuing costs for equipment, the biggest item probably being computer time, are usually included under operation costs, if the equipment is already installed. The "equipment" heading is reserved for one-time purchase or special hardware needed for this system. If, for example, one of the software packages requires adding more core memory to the CPU, its cost would be included here, either as a one-time cost in the first year if it were purchased, or as a continuing cost if leased. Installation and maintenance of the equipment should be included as well. The fact that the extra hardware can be used for other systems in the future should not be taken into account by showing costs lower than they will actually be. The temptation to write off all extra costs this way is too great. The total of these four major items gives the total cost of the system year by year.

Savings are the costs of those parts in the present operation which will be replaced by the computer system. To arrive at this figure it will be necessary to estimate what they would have been if no new systems were installed. If the business is expanding, clerical costs over a five- or seven-year period will inevitably rise, more or less in direct ratio to the increase in paper work. If the work load is increasing and expected to keep on increasing at the rate of 10 percent a year, then if the savings in the first year are $1000, in year 2 they will be $1100, and so on. "Other benefits" are additional profits or reductions in losses that would not occur if no new systems were installed. This might be things like reduction in bad debts, reduction in inventory, or increased sales, but must not include increased sales or other benefits that would occur with or without a new system.

Be realistic about savings. If the new system will save clerical costs of $1800 a year and is installed in November, the saving of $1800 cannot be allocated to that year. Even if the staff is not needed in December, it is best to show no saving until the next year. Fractions of people or machines should not be used. If the present departmental work load can be reduced from 10 to 2½ typists on the basis of the number of hours of work, show savings for a reduction of 7 at most. And if savings are claimed on the seven, the remaining three must be shown as a continuing cost. The sum of savings and other benefits gives the total savings.

The difference between savings and costs each year gives the net balance. It may be negative for the first few years. The discounted cash flow (DCF) factors are applied to the net balance.

For those not initiated into the mysteries of accounting, a short explanation: The figures used in the analysis represent today's money values. The rental for the software might be $2500 each year for five years, fixed by the terms of the contract. But, a dollar in hand this year will very likely have more buying power than a dollar in hand in five years' time. Even if this year's dollar is banked and accumulates interest for five years, at present rates of inflation it would still buy less in five years than it would now. Moreover, the company might be using it; if, instead of investing the $2500 in software, the company put this money into advertising, perhaps the net return would be greater. Also, the figures used in the analysis are estimates at best; the farther into the future they are extended, the less reliable they become because there is an increasing possibility that unforeseen circumstances will arise to make them inaccurate or even meaningless. Discounted cash flow is an educated fudge factor that adjusts the net balance to take these things (and others more esoteric) into account. It is a percentage (decreasing each year) that is deducted from the difference between costs and savings, or added if the balance is negative. (Note that if the five-year cost of renting software equals one-time development cost, DCF favors the software.) It must be applied to the net balance, not to the individual items in the analysis (this is only one method; others are also used).

An example of DCF is shown in Table 7. The actual percentages chosen depend on the state of the economy, company standards, and the number of years covered by the analysis. Always obtain from the company accountants or auditors the figures and details of how percentages should be applied.

TABLE 7. EXAMPLE OF DISCOUNTED CASH FLOW CALCULATIONS

Item	Year 1	Year 2	Year 3	Year 4	Year 5
Net balance	($12,600)	($3,200)	$9,070	$18,400	$29,000
DCF factor	100%	25%	50%	25%	10%
Discounted balance	($25,200)	($5,600)	$13,605	$23,000	$31,000
Cumulative discounted balance	($25,200)	($30,800)	($17,195)	$5,805	$37,705

Cost/Benefit Analysis

A drawback of the methods just discussed is that neither takes full account of the value of intangibles. If one solution is more expensive and also gives extra benefits to which accurate figures cannot be attached, the standard costing methods do not provide all information necessary to make a decision. Cost/benefit analysis by feature is an alternative method.

Consider these situations:

Software	Cost, $	Meets Objectives, %
A	102,000	98
B	120,000	98
A	70,000	98
B	70,000	67

According to this analysis, software A is clearly the choice both times. But now consider

Software	Cost, $	Meets Objectives, %
A	80,000	85
B	90,000	95

Is the extra 10 percent benefit worth an extra $10,000? If all the objectives
are quantifiable in money terms, standard cost analysis will give an answer.
But it is likely that the intangibles will affect this answer. The solution is to
go back to the feature comparison and check software A against software B
point by point to isolate just what it is that the extra cost provides.

Suppose, for example, that the major difference between software A and
software B is that B provides a real-time response to the user's queries, whereas A gives only overnight batch processing. The question becomes one of
whether the faster response is worth $10,000. In real life the differences are
rarely so clear-cut, but in most analyses of this sort they can be narrowed
down sufficiently to allow a balanced decision to be made.

The approach thus suggested is to postpone extensive investigation of the
monetary value of each element of each proposed solution. The objectives
are weighted as described earlier, and comparisons are made on that basis. If
one solution is clearly the best and within the user's price range, well and
good; if not, then a full-scale study can be conducted to estimate the exact
value of the features in which the possible solutions vary—and those only. If
the value of those features cannot be put into dollars and cents, then at least
they have been isolated and can be considered on their other merits.

THE EVALUATION REPORT

The results of the evaluation must be documented. The output of the detailed study and the cost/benefit analysis should be a formal, written report
prepared for user management and data processing management. It can be
considered a detailed feasibility study or post-feasibility study report, a detailed system proposal, or an intermediate step leading up to the development
of systems and programming specifications, or it may delineate contract
negotiations for software, as the case may be.

The report should show to what extent each proposed system will meet the
user's objectives, and how; how much each would cost and what benefits it
would give; particular advantages and disadvantages of each. The tone of the
report as well as the writer's assumption must be that the final decision is
the user's; the report sets out all the information the user needs to make the
decision. The project team may make a recommendation, but all their reasons
must be given in the report, along with supporting information so that the
reader can follow their thinking. As much detail for nonrecommended alternatives should be given as for the recommended one. The material presented up
to the recommendations section should be objective, not subjectively slanted
to bias the reader before he has all the information.

If the user is not well acquainted with data processing jargon, the report must be written in terms he can understand. When software packages are being discussed, remember that every system and especially every software package has its own peculiar vocabulary. To the project team that has analyzed the software, the new terms will have come to sound familiar. This is not so for the user, who, no matter how familiar he is with general data processing terminology, will be lost in a discussion such as

". . . facilitate the revision and/or incremental expansion of data during the system's life cycle. . . ."

". . . record selection criteria includes relational operators, text scan, partial values. . . ."

". . . systems features include multilevel interactive boolean logic retrieval. . . ."

". . . deck-to-capstan movement, read/write head movement and capstan-to-deck movement can be overlapped. . . ."

Three of these examples are from software package descriptions and one is from a technical handbook.

An outline of the contents of an evaluation report is shown in Figure 22. It may be used as a guide for what should be included in a report that must conform in format to installation standards, or it may serve as the format of a table of contents as well as subject matter.

1. Introduction
   Background
   Terms of Reference
   Acknowledgments
   Study Method

2. Objectives
   (as in Fig. 5, item III)

3. Feature Comparison Check Lists

4. System Data (for each system)
   General Description
   Developer
   Background of Software
   Input and Output Samples
   Technical Evaluation Results
   Outline Conversion and Implementation Plan
   Summary of Costs and Benefits
   General Advantages and Disadvantages

5. Recommendations

6. Appendices
   Detailed Cost Breakdowns
   Detailed Savings Breakdowns
   Detailed Implementation Schedule

References

Glossary

FIGURE 22: TYPICAL CONTENTS OF AN EVALUATION REPORT

PART THREE | ACQUISITION

9 | THE CONTRACT

The purchase or lease of almost any software from an outside organization will require the negotiation and signing of a contract. It is here that the systems analyst or data processing manager in charge of the project may feel that he is out of his depth, and become unhappy over the legal jargon offered up. That is not the worst that could happen; contracts for software have been signed almost as an afterthought, leading the company into a bad situation and some unpleasant surprises. This chapter covers the subjects of conducting the negotiation and the possible contract terms, with emphasis on caveats for the buyer. When foreknowledge and common sense are applied, there is no reason why the contract negotiations should not be calm and result in an arrangement that is fair to all parties.

CONTRACT NEGOTIATION

Throughout the evaluation there will have been communication with the suppliers of the packages being considered, up to and including what will become contract terms if that stage is reached. In particular, there will have been discussion about the price, modifications, training, help with installation, and maintenance and other support. So, to that extent, negotiations have already been going on in an informal way, expressed in such terms as "if we were to buy this, what would. . . ." When a decision has been made that, based on operational and cost/benefit factors, one (or several) of the packages can do the job and should be bought if possible, the style changes to the definite future tense: "What will you do for us in the way of. . . ."; and this is the point at which the formal negotiations open.

Some important guidelines for the negotiations are summarized below:

1. Get legal advice from the beginning.

2. Negotiate with a senior person.

3. Negotiate with only one person.

4. Document all verbal agreements.

5. Make sure the contract specifies everything you will get: the prices, the terms, the conditions.

6. Do not announce the final decision until the contract is signed.

7. Remember that no matter what the contract says, success with software depends first of all on a good business relationship between buyer and seller.

Legal Assistance. The first guideline concerns legal assistance. Most software sellers will have a standard contract. If a copy has not already been obtained, get one as soon as formal negotiations begin. Read it carefully and get professional advice on the legal terms. This may come from the company's legal department, if there is one; if not, from the lawyers who usually act for the company. Some experts go so far as to suggest that a lawyer should be a member of the evaluation team (4). There are still not very many lawyers who are thoroughly familiar with computer and software terminology, so it may be necessary to explain the technical terms and the implications of the software purchase. The explanations of the aspects of software contracts in this chapter are not intended to be formal legal advice, but instead are general discussions of the possible implications for successful installation and use of software.

Choice of Seller's Representative. Negotiate with only one person, the most senior one possible. Obviously, the bigger the purchase and the smaller the supplier, the more likely it is that a very senior person will be involved. He will be able to make decisions on the spot, thus saving time and the possibility of last-minute changes because of misunderstandings. Throughout the evaluation and the negotiations, get all agreements in writing. If a salesman has said that so many days of help at installation time will be included in the price, a factor used in the evaluation, get it in writing from him at the time to avoid later disappointment. During formal meetings on the contract, take notes of what is agreed, review them verbally at the end of the meeting, and put them in a letter to the supplier immediately afterward. He should confirm them in writing without delay.

Documentation. Everything that has been agreed should be in the contract, even if it means expanding or revising the standard form. There will usually be some phrase to the effect that the contract constitutes the whole of the agreement between the two parties; it should include all items agreed upon, whether or not they have previously been put in writing. The letters exchanged during negotiations are not sufficient. An exception to this might be a contract reference to system and program specifications, to define the system. The documentation itself does not have to be a part of the contract as long as all elements are named and described in enough detail to leave no doubt about what is meant.

Timing the Announcement. Do not announce the final choice, or informally let other competitors know about it, until the contract has actually been signed. It is always possible that something could go wrong at the last minute, and the company might want to resort to another supplier. A precipitative announcement limits flexibility of choice.

SPECIAL DEALS

It may be possible to make a special arrangement with the supplier in the form of reduction in package price, special modifications, extra installation help, or whatever is needed most. Particularly if the package is still under development, the supplier will be open to suggestions. If he is feeling the pinch of development costs, he may be anxious for some firm sales. These possibilities are not quite so common as in the early days of software, but when conferring with a small company about a new package it is worth a try. The most obvious arrangement is the supplier's offer of development help because assistance is more likely to involve computer time rather than programmers. The arrangement for the purchaser might be a reduction in the price in exchange for so many hours of time; or, for the supplier, the sale of time at a low cost. If an agreement is reached, get it specified in writing that if the company agrees to buy this package, then . . . and so on. Clearly state everything so that there will be no later misunderstandings—what shift the time is to be on, who supplies the operators, number of hours, and so on.

Some software houses welcome the assistance of potential buyers at specification time. One project control package was developed in this way. The developer felt that he would have a more marketable product if users assisted in the specifications. Accordingly, three companies were invited to become "sponsors." They participated in design sessions, donated machine time, and permitted use of their names for advertising. In return, they got the finished system at a low rate and a royalty on all subsequent sales. In addition, they got the next best thing to a tailored package because they were sure that their own particular requirements were accommodated.

The other major area in which help may be offered in return for some advantage is marketing. It could range from letting the company name be used as a buyer, through talking to potential buyers after the system is installed, to giving demonstrations for prospects on the company's computer. If the arrangement is likely to require the time of staff or computer, be sure it is agreed in advance what it will amount to and how it will be distributed. Again, spell it all out in writing, whatever it may be; say, not more than one demonstration or visit a week at 4 P.M. on Thursdays. Include a termination clause; it would be best to set both an absolute time limit and a notice period; for example, that the arrangement can be terminated by the company on two weeks' notice.

Whether or not it is officially agreed, however, as a matter of courtesy a buyer should be willing to talk to others who are considering the package, if only on the telephone, especially if he has had the same help from other users in his own evaluation.

Some software houses offer a free trial period for certain software. Obviously, this is not feasible for systems requiring the establishment of a large data base, but it may be available for programmer aides and utility programs. If this offer is accepted, play fair; if it's good, keep it and enter into contract; if not, return all documentation *uncopied*.

It is important that dickering for a special deal be done before formal contract negotiations are entered—in fact, before the detailed evaluation takes place. After the first round of information gathering, inform each supplier on the short list that a more detailed evaluation will take place. Ask him to specify now what special deals or discounts he is prepared to offer. These can then be taken into account during the evaluation, not in a mad scramble to revise the cost analysis after the final decision is supposed to have been made.

Do not play one supplier off against another in an attempt to get a better deal. The "can you top this" game is usually played by the head of the company negotiating team, who phones salesman Y to tell him that salesman X has just offered a 10 percent discount and an extra week of help with file conversion and free modifications; what does salesman Y have to say about that? It sometimes works, but those who finally get the business feel they have the worst end of the deal or have been outmaneuvered. This cannot lead to a good relationship during installation and the possibly many years of give-and-take to come. The small financial advantage gained is not worth the risk of damaging what would otherwise be good terms between the two companies and the individuals who have worked together to get the software installed and keep it running.

The ethics of the situation cut both ways. In one case known to the author, the head of a selection team was told by one salesman that there would be a "substantial rebate" if the contract was signed within the next few days, and that the "rebate" would be cash paid directly to the team leader and never mentioned officially. This is a bribe, no matter how worded, and as a result that company was immediately struck from the list of those under consideration.

Scrupulously avoid any under-the-table deals or personal arrangements. The risk is too great, and even if such deals never come to light, there will be inevitable tension, deteriorating morale, and loss of respect on both sides. Signing the contract is only the beginning. The software has to be installed and maintained, which means a business relationship continuing for many years. No matter what it says in the contract, the success or failure of the venture depends on individuals in the two companies being on good working terms.

THE PACKAGE

The contract should contain a description of what the package comprises. First of all, the programs should be named with reference to the documentation and system descriptions already received. It should specify in what form the programs will be delivered—source program on cards, object program on tape, or whatever—and that they will be compatible with the systems software and the hardware to be used. The documentation should be specified, along with the number of copies of each document to be provided. Any special equipment that is part of the package should be designated.

The package usually comprises more than just programs. The training to be supplied should be spelled out, including who will do it, who is to be trained, how many days of training there will be, and the scheduling of instruction sessions. If any new forms are required, their type, number, and responsibility for supply should be mentioned.

The contract should contain some statement from the supplier that the package is his to sell, and that if any disputes arise over ownership, the purchaser, as a third party, will not be liable for any claims.

The buyer's right to use the package should also be spelled out. What if more than one computer is installed within the company? What if they are at different locations? What happens if the computer is down and the user wants to use the software on a machine located externally?

PRICES AND PAYMENTS

The price of a packaged system may have little to do with its value to the buyer. If offered by a private organization—another user—its philosophy may be that it would have had to develop it anyway and any money they make by selling it is "gravy." Some give away systems for the cost of copying the documentation, but of course no training or other support can then be expected.

A software house (and as pointed out earlier, manufacturers are beginning to be included in this category) faces a dilemma. Theoretically, the lower the price, the more they will sell, but the longer it will take to get back development costs and start making a profit. Most houses set the price by estimating how many they can sell, then divide their total costs by that, and add a percentage for profit. This is usually done before the system is developed, and the estimates may be unduly optimistic. As the expected number of buyers declines and development and marketing costs go up, the price of the package goes up too. On one project control package, for example, the price more than doubled between the time it was announced and the first delivery (early buyers got a bargain). The cost of one well-known, generalized file processor has almost doubled since the first sales were made, partly because of improvements and partly because the software house grossly underestimated the amount of installation support needed.

Even on the first sale of a package, usually less than half the price goes toward development costs; the remainder is for marketing, documentation, training, and other support. Some of the popular lower-priced programmer aids, like flowcharters, have sold so well that development costs were recovered fairly quickly and the packages have turned into miniature gold mines for their developers—the better mousetrap.

From the point of view of the software house, however, the number of buyers is not necessarily inversely related to the price. In one informal survey, a number of data processing managers were shown bare details of several competing packages. Asked to choose which they would buy if no more information were available, most picked the highest priced package. When asked why, the universal response was: "If it's that expensive it must be good."

From the buyer's point of view, as was pointed out in an earlier chapter, the price of the package may be considerably lower than if he had done the system himself. But a number of contract caveats affect the price and method of payment and may offset this apparent discrepancy.

Type of Acquisition

There are two basic forms of software acquisition, purchase and lease, and either should be clearly stated. If it is an outright sale, the contract will probably forbid reselling or giving it away. Be careful about the terms of installment payments—a company is committed to buying the package and paying all money from the time the contract is signed, even if it stops using the software before it has finished paying.

Leasing is becoming more popular. The payments are usually scheduled on an annual basis, with an option for renewal of the contract when it expires.

The schedule for installment payments, or the terms of a lease, is linked to events rather than to calendar dates: delivery of the package, satisfactory completion of the acceptance test, and so on. The length of the lease ranges from one year to seven or more. When the lease expires or is terminated by either party (discussed later), all copies of the programs, documentation, etc., must be returned.

Responsibility for payment of any sales taxes due should be specifically assigned. This is one area in which the services of a lawyer are especially necessary because of different interpretations of various laws, and because legal implications are likely to change in relation to software. The company accountants will also be interested in the possibility of tax write-offs. Davis and Blose (22) said that the U.S. Internal Revenue Service has no conclusive ruling with respect to tax allowances for software depreciation:

> As far as purchased software costs are concerned, the tax treatment of allowing a write-off over five years or less appears very reasonable, since, with any asset, it is necessary to establish an actual life. The only problem would be in proving a shorter life. The alternative treatment of purchased software costs (separate or included), allows the taxpayer a degree of flexibility but is somewhat uncertain and its value depends on the progress the computer industry makes toward unbundling.

In the United Kingdom and Europe, the full effects of the value-added tax system (VAT) are not yet known. If it is necessary to pay VAT on cremated bodies in Europe,[1] it is likely that software in England will be taxed in this way too.

DELIVERY AND INSTALLATION

Delivery and installation are not single events, but the culmination of a number of events. Get them defined in the contract. Does "delivery" mean the physical presence of the programs at the buyer's installation, or all associated documentation and compilation of programs, or everything included in the package? It should be the latter. If it has been agreed that modifications will be made, these must be specified whether they are to be done before or after delivery.

Installation of the software may refer to the first run, whether successful or not, or to the first successful operational run, something in between, or

[1] From *The Observer*, Jan. 23, 1972.

something else entirely. Make sure everyone knows what is meant and who has what responsibilities. If programs have to be compiled, who is responsible for supervising the work, the company's staff or the supplier's? Find out how much machine time is required, and make sure it is available on the time and day called for. The time the supplier will give to support installation should be specified, along with the facilities for his staff.

MODIFICATIONS, MAINTENANCE, AND IMPROVEMENTS

Modifications

If the supplier has agreed to special modifications to make the software fit special requirements, be certain these are documented as soon as they are agreed upon. It should then be stated in the contract exactly what comprises each modification (with reference to any specifications which exist), who is responsible for design, programming, testing, computer time, and other expenses, and when the modifications will be completed. If the sale is dependent on the success of an acceptance test, the test should include the modifications, and this should be made clear in the contract.

Maintenance

As used in a software contract, maintenance usually means keeping the system running to the original specification; therefore it includes debugging, changes to accommodate changes by the manufacturer in the compiler or operating system, and possible changes to comply with legal requirements (for example, a new tax law). It does not usually include changes to increase efficiency, facilitate use, or adjust to demands of an unstable business environment. The contract should clearly state who is responsible for each type.

If system maintenance is the supplier's responsibility, then its cost should be allocated either as part of the purchase price or as an extra charge. Usually it is included. If it is extra, the charge rate should be specified, as well as the terms and conditions. The latter should include the response time to the buyer's request for maintenance (especially important in the early stages of a new system, when bugs are likely to appear), the maximum time to implementation of the fix, who provides machine time for testing, and responsibility for updating documentation.

Improvements

The second category of maintenance, changes that are desirable but not necessarily essential, come under the heading of "improvements." They may be initiated by the software user or by the supplier. The contract should deal with both possibilities. Is the buyer allowed to make such modifications himself? If so, who owns them? Do they belong exclusively to the buyer or can the supplier appropriate them to incorporate in other versions of the package? If so, does he pay or not? How much? Suppose the buyer does alter the programs, is the supplier still responsible for the first category of maintenance? The answer to that is usually no, for understandable reasons: It is unfair to require the supplier to commit his resources to a problem whose proportion is not known. The user's "tampering" with the programs might have to be undone, or may so change them that other maintenance becomes extremely time consuming. For the peace of mind of all, the usual stipulation is either that the supplier does all maintenance, or none of it.

The situation with regard to improvements made on the supplier's own initiative should be also defined. Is the purchaser entitled to have these free, or does he have to pay? Over a period of years the accumulated improvements could amount to a complete revision of the system. One common arrangement is to include in the original price all improvements made for the first two years or so, if the buyer wants them. After that, the system remains static unless the buyer wants to replace the contract with a new one for a new version, probably at a higher price. If a company is to get regular modifications and improvements, be sure the contract states who is going to have the job of updating the documentation.

Nondisclosure and Copyright

Ever since proprietary software was first marketed, software houses have had the problem of how to protect their product (which could represent many years of work and a large investment) from being stolen, either by users who would otherwise buy it or by an unscrupulous competitor. (In fact, any computer user who develops systems should be alert to this possibility, especially if the unauthorized use of one of his systems by a competitor could give the competitor an advantage he would not otherwise have.) There are four possible methods of protecting the originator against such piracy: patents, trade secret, copyright, or contractual agreements.

Patent applications for computer programs have only recently been allowed in the United States. Few applications have been made and fewer granted. There has been much discussion over whether programs are inventions, that is, a new process or apparatus. As the patent law is presently interpreted and applied, it apparently does not offer any practical protection for software.

The status of trade secret protection for software has been summarized well by Robert Head. "The possessor of a trade secret has long had protection available to him under the common law. If he can demonstrate that he does possess a valuable trade secret, others can be prevented from obtaining and using that secret." (32) The owner of a package can try to obtain both kinds, copyright and trade secret protection, by distinguishing between sales literature and postsale documentation. Sales literature may consist of advertising materials, general descriptions, samples of output, and so on, which are sent out wholesale to possible buyers. This material may be copyrighted. Postsale documentation includes such things as the user manual, operating instructions, and the like, which would be specified 'confidential' and handed over to the customer only when the contract has been finalized and signed.

Copyright does not protect the use of the material, but prohibits copying all or any part of it and declares such appropriation to be an infringement. A copyright cannot be obtained on an idea, only on its expression. For example, if a cartographer wanted to publish a map of Houston, Texas, and all existing maps were copyrighted, he would have to do the survey and draw his own map. It might look just like all other maps, but as long as he had done all the work himself and had not copied another map, he would not be infringing on any copyright and could obtain one himself.

In the United States, protection for certain classes[2] of *unpublished work* is extended through statutory copyright by registering one copy with the Copyright Office. Once published, it must show the notice of copyright and be registered by depositing two copies (in the case of programs, two listings) with the Copyright Office. This means that program listings and all documentation can be copyrighted. Making any copy of it by hand or machine (except for certain literary purposes, such as a short quote in a book or a book review) would be an infringement.

Almost any software documentation obtainable from a software house, including sales literature and program listing, will probably have the copyright symbol "©" on it. If it does, copies of any kind for any reason cannot be made unless the user has permission in writing from the copyright holder. If copies will be needed for internal distribution and for backup, it is a good idea to get permission granted right in the contract. Unbundled IBM program products are copyrighted. IBM has stated, for example, that it would regard computer translation from PL/1 to COBOL as an infringement.

The situation is very similar in the United Kingdom, although patenting is even less a possibility at present. A government committee has recommended that computer programs not be patentable because it might restrict the free

---

[2]Certain classes of unpublished material *cannot* be registered. Refer to Title 17 of the United States Code.

dissemination of ideas and inhibit the growth of the industry. In any case, it can take up to three years and cost £500 ($1250) to get a patent, which is bound to discourage most software houses. Copyright is easier because no registration is required. The copyright applies in all member countries of the Berne Copyright Union, which includes almost every country in the world except the United States, Soviet Union, China, and some South American countries.

Many standard software contracts contain a *secrecy* or *nondisclosure clause*. Read it carefully. If the supplier agrees, remove it. If he insists on including it, make sure that it covers only programs and documented material, not anything told orally. Make sure it does not cover data or any material (such as invoices) to be sent out of the company. (One company found itself in the onerous position of not being able to show its own data to any outsider because the contract contained a secrecy agreement covering the software that processed the data.) Be sure that there is no restriction on making backup copies of the documentation and the program, or on rewriting the documentation if needed. If the company has a backup arrangement with an outside installation, be sure it will be permitted to run the system there and to take along the programs and operating instructions. If operators other than company employees will run the system under any circumstances, special permission may be needed for that, too. If temporaries are sometimes hired as computer operators or in any other area (e.g., the user department) where they might need to use the manuals, check to be sure that this is allowed. Also, make certain that if use of the software is terminated, it can be replaced with another package or with an in-house system.

Some suppliers insist upon a secrecy clause and will not sell the system without it, for understandable reasons. If the contract signed includes it, the company has the responsibility to make sure that all employees who come into contact with the system know about it. They may not discuss details with an outsider, "lend" the documentation to a friendly programmer in another installation, or take any of the documentation with them if they leave for another job. Management has the responsibility to control program listings and documentation to make sure that no staff member has the opportunity to make unauthorized copies. If there is a violation, the company will be liable.

PENALTIES

A penalty clause may impose fines in the case of late delivery or failure to perform to specification, or both. The fine may be a lump sum or a per diem reduction from the price until the terms of the contract are met. The only things that may make the clause inoperative might be Acts of God or circumstances not under the seller's control. Penalties are, naturally enough, not part of any standard contract, but are usually imposed at the insistence of the buyer.

There is much to be said against the use of penalties. First of all, collection can be a time-consuming and expensive process, especially if it is necessary to go to court. It just may not be worth the time and the effort. In any case, the presence of the clause, and the negotiations that led up to its insertion, could generate such an atmosphere of mutual distrust and antagonism that the implementation would be rougher than it need be. The buyer's staff would be cast in the role of policemen and judges, suspiciously scrutinizing every move made by the supplier's staff, who in turn would be looking for every possible excuse to cast any blame for delays on the buyer's staff. Suppliers have been known to go to extreme lengths to avoid paying crippling penalties, up to and including fake and real nervous breakdowns of the project manager (to gain sympathy and compassionate waiver of the penalty) and sabotage of the reputations of user staff (so the blame can be put on them). The buyer's staff, on the other hand, may be tempted by the thought of a cheap system and try to delay the project surreptitiously. With a very heavy penalty hanging over the project, the quibbling and backbiting that goes on in such a situation has to be seen to be believed.

The insertion of a penalty clause should always be done reluctantly and as a last resort. There are some special situations where it may be desirable. For instance, if the seller has a good product and a unique one (there is no other possible supplier nor a similar system nearly so good), but the company has a history of late delivery, then a penalty in this case may be warranted. (A better solution might be to motivate him with a bonus for early delivery.) Another case might be where installation of the system is necessary to comply with legal requirements or meet an essential company deadline, when failure to get on the air would mean serious difficulties and financial loss for the buyer. The penalty then would be compensatory rather than punitive.

A justification for penalties for nonperformance might be that the software house, for security reasons, has refused to reveal enough detailed information to make a full-scale evaluation possible. The penalty specified should be reasonable—more for compensation than punishment, and not a figure so ridiculously high that the supplier would go out of business if he had to pay (collecting it would be very difficult). It is not fair to ask for a heavy penalty as a put-up or shut-up measure, as some companies have been known to do to test the supplier's confidence in his product and his ability to deliver it. If the supplier were foolish enough to accept, the kind of conflict situation described earlier might arise, to nobody's benefit. If a company is that doubtful of the seller, either his evaluation has not been thorough enough or he should not be doing business with that supplier in the first place.

LIABILITY

Every contract has a standard clause stating that in the case of damage to equipment or data, the seller will not be liable beyond the price of the software. If something should go wrong and the master files unto the fourth generation were wiped out, the cost to the vendor company would be horrendous, for it would have to re-create the data and compensate for loss of business plus loss of a processing system, at the least—assuming that it could re-create the data at all. Lesser disasters could still be expensive, to an order of magnitude greater than the refund price of the package.

From the seller's point of view, no sane person with experience in data processing would bet his company's life on the fact that there were no bugs left in the best-tested system. The limitation of liability clause is absolutely necessary as insurance against freak combinations of circumstances or sheer bad luck. Of course, if a supplier's system did do a large amount of damage to a client, the bad publicity might well drive him out of business anyway, especially if he were small. The software business as it is today could not exist without the limitation of liability clause. It is there and it is going to stay there, regardless of how much it makes the buyer wince.

TERMINATION

If the software is being leased, one section of the contract should deal with the circumstances of termination. For a bought package, if maintenance is done on a per-year charge, similar conditions will need to be put in. It should cover reasons for termination by the buyer or by the seller, and the method.

A lease may be indefinite, monthly, or automatically annually renewable unless one party takes some action, or it may be for a fixed length of time measured in months or years. For the buyer's protection, he should be able to terminate at any time, given a reasonable notice period, merely by officially informing the supplier in writing that he wishes to do so. No reason need be given. On the other hand, the supplier may be willing to pledge support and continued availability of the package for a term of years, barring Acts of God or circumstances beyond his control. If the package represents a major capital investment both in the software cost and in setting up and running the system, he may want this protection. Moreover, the supplier may want an escape route if the client proves unreasonably demanding or troublesome. Whatever the final agreement, it should be specified in the contract.

Another desirable clause in the contract is one that guarantees performance in case the supplier becomes inactive. What happens if he is acquired by another company or goes out of business? What happens if he decides to stop supporting the package? What if he sells all his rights in it to someone else? In some cases an automatic purchase clause might be the answer, but each case should be decided on the circumstances.

SUMMARY

Figures 23 and 24 summarize this discussion of contract terms, although they are organized somewhat differently from the text, setting out contract terms as applicable to protection for the buyer and protection for the seller. Notice that a number of items appear on both lists; that is no mistake. The contract is a two-way document. Its purpose is not to give an advantage to one party or the other but to set out the conditions of the agreement in such a way that there can be no misunderstanding. It is through misunderstandings and misinterpretations that unpleasant situations arise. If the acquisition of software is to be a successful venture, the software house and the buying company must be able to work together.

THE PACKAGE
  What it includes
  Reference to specifications
  Ownership, copyright, third
    party claims
  Usage
THE TERMS
  Whether sale or lease
  Price
  Method of payment
  Time scale of payment (tied to
    events, not the calendar)
  Discounts
  Taxes
  Definitions of "delivery" and
    "installation"
  Responsibilities for installation
DOCUMENTATION
  What it consists of
  When it will be delivered
  How many copies
  Permission to make additional
    copies
  Permission to write own manuals

MODIFICATIONS/MAINTEN-
ANCE/IMPROVEMENTS
  Terms; what and at what cost
  Responsibilities
  Ownership
  Delivery dates
  Service
  Expenses
PENALTIES
  Reasons
  Time scale
  Recovery
TERMINATION
  Reasons and method
  Liabilities
  If seller goes out of business
  If package rights disposed of
  Replacement of package

FIGURE 23: PROTECTION FOR THE BUYER: CONTRACT TERMS

147

THE PACKAGE
  What it includes
  Reference to specifications
  Ownership
  Usage
THE TERMS
  Whether sale or lease
  Price and method of payment
  Taxes
  Definitions of "delivery" and
    "installation"
  Responsibilities
  Limitation of liability
  Right to make alterations

INSTALLATION
  Responsibilities
  Preparation by buyer
  Acceptable reasons for late
    delivery
COPYRIGHT AND PATENTS
  Specification of what copyright
    covers
  Specification of what patents
    cover
  Copying privilege exclusion
NONDISCLOSURE CLAUSE
  What is covered
  Responsibilities of buyer
  Penalties

FIGURE 24: PROTECTION FOR THE SELLER: CONTRACT TERMS

10 | THE ACCEPTANCE TEST

An acceptance test for software is simply a systems test. On its outcome depends the final decision of whether or not this software is suitable. Mechanically it does not differ very much from a garden-variety system test of an in-house developed system. This chapter does not go into the detail of those mechanics, which should be nothing new for the experienced systems analyst, but instead will concentrate on the differences in approach and management of a software acceptance test.

Thinking and planning should have begun in the early stages of the selection project, just as planning for an ordinary systems test has to begin long before programming.

REASONS FOR ELIMINATING ACCEPTANCE TESTS

The first decision is whether an acceptance test is necessary at all. Some types of software may not require it in some circumstances. The considerations in favor of skipping an acceptance test are:

1. The package is inexpensive to buy or lease, to install, and to run.
2. If the package is leased, the terms of the contract are such that it can be terminated on short notice.
3. There is a free trial period (an acceptance test in effect if not in name).
4. The software is not performing essential functions for which there is no alternative.
5. The package has a proven history of success.

Obviously, software that meets most of these five criteria will usually be pro-

grammer aides and utility programs. Take, for example, a source deck cataloging and updating system. Prices for these range from $250 to several thousand
for an outright purchase, or $75 to $100 per month leased, and sometimes
less. All but brand-new installations will already have some method for amend-
ing and storing source decks—the department will not go out of business without the package.

The selection project is a small-scale one. Say an analyst is assigned to it,
writes away for detailed information on a half-dozen systems, set up his criteria check lists, and goes back to three of the companies with more questions.
He makes phone calls to a few of their clients, picks the system that seems to
best fit the hardware and the particular requirements of the installation, and
writes a short report for the data processing manager who approves his recommendation. The terms are $80 a month rental, termination on a month's
notice, maintenance included. Previous customers report satisfaction, and the
specifications are detailed and clear. The whole thing has taken less than a
week of the analyst's time, if he is efficient.

Is an acceptance test worthwhile? Probably not. The first few weeks of
operation will prove whether the system does what was claimed by the seller.
If it does not, the lease can be terminated without paying more than the first
month's $80. An acceptance test would cost more than that in setting up
test data. Problems could arise only if backup copies of the source programs
entrusted to the new system were not kept—any installation without the
basic common sense to do that does not have enough expertise to do an acceptance test anyway.

REASONS FOR REQUIRING ACCEPTANCE TESTS

The considerations in favor of doing an acceptance test are:

1. The package is expensive.
2. Operation requires the establishment of a large data base.
3. The contract is binding for a long period of time.
4. The system will be performing essential functions that the company cannot do without.
5. The system has not been operational in another installation.

Large-scale packages like generalized file processors and applications packages, particularly newly developed ones, meet these criteria. The basic rule
here can be expressed as: If there is no looking back, do an acceptance test.
Consider an insurance policy processing system for a million policies, which

costs $150,000 to buy or $5,000 a month to lease. Setting up the files, producing all the new forms required, training users, and so on could cost as much as another $150,000. In that situation there should be absolutely no hesitation about whether to do an acceptance test.

Given the nature of the problem at feasibility study time, the necessity for an acceptance test will have been obvious. Suppliers should be told from the start that test results will be a deciding factor. When the choice has been made and contract negotiations begin, it must not come as a surprise to the supplier that the sale will not be final until the tests are evaluated and proved satisfactory.

ACCEPTANCE TEST DATA

The User's Requirements

It will be necessary to develop test data. The problems of doing this are just the same as those for an in-house system, but they incur a more stringent requirement: test cases must be comprehensive, covering *every possible* situation. The project team will not necessarily need to know how the processing is carried out. In fact, it may be well if it does not, for then there is no possibility of biasing the choice of test cases toward those the system handles best.

It is necessary to know the types of inputs and the options, and what outputs should look like. For each test case, then, the team develops the input and specifies what output should result. (Output here includes master file records, etc., as well as reports and other printed output.) There are obvious reasons why this must be done by the project team, using realistic samples, and not by the supplier. The supplier will, of course, have to give details of input, file layouts, and output to make this possible. The test plan, covering number of test runs, test cases for each, scheduling, responsibilities, and so on, should be developed by the project team too.

All this preparation has to be done before the contract is actually signed. The contract should specify that the acquisition is dependent on the results of the test, and the test cases and plan should be attached to it or at least specifically described. It must go further than that. Who judges the results? What performance level is satisfactory? Project the possible results of the acceptance test. Supposing that 80 percent of the output is as expected and 20 percent is either in error or not as specified. Is that good enough? Perhaps the supplier will argue that since a substantial number of the cases were right, therefore the system as a whole has passed the test. The buyer does not agree because the company could not operate well with that grade of results. It will be very difficult to settle the disagreement unless it is spelled out in the contract how much, and which, of the test cases have to be satisfactory for the system as a whole to be acceptable.

Suppose again that everyone agrees, and it is written into the contract that the results must be 100 percent as specified in the test output samples attached to the contract. Then the test results show only 95 percent right, but the supplier says, "OK, fine, we'll get that fixed up for you right away." Decide what is to be done in a situation like that before it happens, and get agreement on it. If the results are substantially satisfactory, it does seem reasonable to give the software house a chance to adjust the remaining problems. But the buyer should not be backed into giving the vendor what amounts to free computer time and checkout help to test and debug the system. The acceptance test is for the user's benefit, not the sellers. It would be well to get it written into the contract that any machine time needed for alterations at this stage will be paid for by the seller and at a specified rate; allow for the possibility in scheduling the conversion.

The difficulty faced by a number of software buyers in situations similar to the one described above is that, having come this far, continuing with the debugging and retesting almost indefinitely seems easier and cheaper than to throw the rascals out and go to number two on the list. A systematic and thorough evaluation before the acceptance test stage is reached is the only way to avoid this problem. Too many users remember with bitterness and resentment the problems they had with early software from the manufacturers, who released it too early and called the resulting chaos "field testing." Where there is a choice of software, keen competition between suppliers, and the option of doing it in house, such pandemonium is not necessary.

If a company is the first buyer of a package and it has reason to believe that an acceptance test would develop into a whole series of tests, the best course might be to ask the supplier to give a frank appraisal of this work. Suggest that the final testing and debugging of the system be a joint venture between the company and him. Of course the buyer would expect a reduction in the price (see Chapter 9, "Special Deals"). A cooperative venture is possible only if the buyer has spare capacity and can wait for the system.

The testing should be conducted by the company's own staff all the way. The best policy is to keep the supplier's people off the premises altogether, unless a problem arises.

The Supplier's Obligations

Acceptance test time provides an opportunity for evaluating things other than the system itself. If something goes wrong, or questions arise during the test, make a note of the response the supplier gives. Does he have someone on the spot as fast as he said he could? Note the level of competence of the individuals sent.

Some companies go so far as to set up situations that test the response and support given. The promptness with which a call brings help and how fast and how cheerfully the problem is solved are indications of the day-to-day support that will be forthcoming once the sale is final. Of course, it is possible that the service could get worse, but it is certain that it will never be any better.

SUMMARY

In summary, then, the important considerations for acceptance testing are to plan it well in advance; anticipate all possible results; get the conditions of the test written into the contract, making the final acquisition dependent on success of the test; and get advance agreement on interpretation of the results.

APPENDIX A | SOURCES OF INFORMATION

APPENDIX A.
Sources
of Information

Sources of information listed in this Appendix are presented in two categories, subscription or catalog services and periodic professional publications.

INFORMATION SERVICES

ICP Quarterly. Subscribers to this service receive quarterly catalogs containing brief descriptions of programs for sale, including machine, price, and name and address to contact for further information. The only requirement for a listed program is that it be documented and/or supported so as to be operational. If the user cannot find a program to suit his requirements in the catalog, ICP will do a search at no additional charge. Subscription cost is $100.00 per year and requests for the service may be addressed to any one of the following centers:

International Computer Programs, Inc., 2511 East 46th St., Indianapolis, Indiana 46205
Prodata International GMBH, 6 Frankfurt am Main, Eschersheimer Landstrasse 60, Germany
Techno System Corporation, Yaesu 5-5 Building 5-5, Yaesu, Chou-Ko, Tokyo, Japan
Wennergren-Williams A.B., Nordenflychtsvagen 70, Stockholm, Sweden

AUERBACH Software Reports. This service publishes detailed reports and comparison charts on packages by application area, including inventory control, payroll, accounts receivable, accounts payable, general ledger, information storage and retrieval, flowcharting and documentation, file maintenance, and production planning and control. The full service includes reference guides, software overview, hardware requirements summary, introduction to programming languages, and bimonthly updates to the application modules. Subscription prices are $490 per year for the full set, $90 for an individual application module, without updates, and $95 for individual modules sent outside the United States. Make inquiries to:

AUERBACH Associates Inc., 121 N. Broad St., Philadelphia, Pa. 19107
AUERBACH Publishers Inc., Davis House, 69/77 High Street, Croydon CR9
    1QH, England

Business Automation Product Information Services–Software Edition. The service includes software package abstracts, state-of-the-art reports, specialized software package reviews, and monthly updates. Cost is $85 the first year and $50 renewal thereafter. A trial subscription is offered for $10. Write to:

Business Automation Product Information Services, Hitchcock Publishing
    Company, Hitchcock Building, Wheaton, Illinois 60187

CIC Information Service. This is a subscription service that provides a monthly information catalog, query answering service, private study facilities, and market research. Publications cover hardware, software, service bureaus, publications, agencies, etc. Its main facility is based in England, but it covers computer science worldwide. The price depends on the type of user and size of installation. Average cost is £150 per year. Send inquiries to:

Computer Information Centre Ltd., 286-288 Pentonville Road, London N.1.,
    England

Co-Pac Index. This information service covers software, service bureaus, time-sharing bureaus, computer time for hire, and computer training courses. Subscription includes a yearbook updated every eight weeks, plus current awareness service for information on a particular subject as received. It is of interest primarily to United Kingdom users. Price is £25 per year. Special inquiries cost £1 per item for subscribers. For information, write to:

Co-Pac Index Ltd., 17 Princess Street Harrigate, Yorkshire HG1 1NG, England

The NCC National Computer Program Index. This service is open to all. An inquiry specifying the type of system being sought is answered by abstracts giving a narrative description, machine and peripherals needed, and who to contact for more information. Information is free. Address:

The Information Officer, The National Computing Centre, Quay House, Quay Street, Manchester 3M3 3HU, England

DECUS Program Library Catalog. This catalog has extensive listings of programs obtainable from PDP users, and is organized by PDP computer type. It is maintained by the Digital Equipment Computer Users Society, and is available to both members and interested nonusers free of charge. Write to:

DECUS Program Library Catalog, 146 Maynard St., Maynard, Massachusetts 01754

PERIODICALS

The periodicals mentioned below are only a few of the hundreds of magazines and newspapers serving the data processing community. Chapter 4 contains a general discussion about research using periodicals as source material.

EDP Analyzer. Each issue covers a single topic of interest to computer users. Software subjects in the past have included generalized packages, software selection, independent software companies, data management, etc. Back issues are available. The publication is independent and accepts no advertising. Subscription price is $36 per year (monthly), or $5 per single issue. Address: EDP Analyzer, 134 Escondido Av., Vista, California 92083.

Software Practice and Experience. Offers articles on software design and implementation, and case studies; also has a regular feature on computer games. Aimed at the software writer, but should be of interest to users as well. International in scope. Quarterly. Price: $23.40 per year in United States, £8.50 per year in United Kingdom. Address: John Wiley & Sons Ltd., Baffins Lane, Chichester, Sussex, England.

Software World. This magazine has articles on software topics, plus listings of packages for sale. Quarterly. Price: $25.00 per year in United States; £8.40 per year in the United Kingdom. Subscriptions include a monthly newsletter. Address: Software World, Morley House, 26-30 Holborn Viaduct, London E.C.1., England.

Software Digest. Publishes news on programming developments, markets, etc. Weekly. Price: United States, Canada, Mexico: $75 per year, $40 per six months; other areas, $100 per year. Address: EPD News Services, 514 10th Street, N.W., Washington, D.C. 20004.

APPENDIX B

AUTOMATED TECHNIQUES FOR PROGRAM EVALUATION

APPENDIX B.
Automated Techniques
for Program Evaluation

The systems described in this Appendix are representative samples of those available. Most were developed with the primary objective of improving program performance, but they can be used for evaluation alone. For a further discussion, see Chapter 7.

SYSTEMS MEASUREMENT SOFTWARE

There are a number of products in the SMS/360 line, but the one of interest here is called Problem Program Efficiency (PPE). It consists of two programs, the extractor and the analyzer, which do just what their names imply. The extractor is resident with the program being observed during an operational run, and samples its activity. An interval timer is required, and the problem program is excluded from using it. The analyzer is then run on the data collected, producing the Code Activity Report (CAR). The report includes, among other things, the distribution of executed instructions, distribution of wait time, percentage time spent executing SVC's (supervisors' calls) subreports on selected modules of the program, and a histogram showing percentage of execution time by groups of instruction or even by individual instructions. It is thus possible to identify the parts of the program using the most time, in order to examine the instructions to see whether they are inefficient. The price is $6,000 in the United States and £2,500 in the United Kingdom. Suppliers include:

Boole & Babbage, Inc., 1121 San Antonio Road, Palo Alto, California 94303
Computer Analysts & Programmers, Ltd., CAP House, 14-15 Great James
    Street, London W.C.1., England

LAMBDA EFFICIENCY ANALYSIS PROGRAM

LEAP is a resident monitor to be run in conjunction with the program being evaluated. It is available for IBM 360 and 370 OS, BAL, FORTRAN, COBOL, and PL/1. It monitors and analyzes in one job step, and reports on time distribution, subroutine calls, CPU utilization, channel use and overlap, queues, device usage, and operating system usage. Price is $8500. Available from the Lambda Corporation, 1501 Wilson Blvd., Arlington, Virginia 22209.

SYSTEMS AND COMPUTERS EVALUATION AND REVIEW TECHNIQUE

The SCERT system simulates applications under various hardware/software configurations, and can therefore be used to test the same application under a variety of software and hardware combinations, or to test different applications systems on the same hardware/software. A mathematical model of the processes is built and a simulation is conducted. The system is updated regularly for new hardware and software. For program efficiency review, SCERT makes specific recommendations for improvement. The system can be leased on a time basis, or a per-job basis, and SCERT consultants do the work, or train the user, depending on the requirements of the job. Prices are therefore dependent on the nature of the work to be done. Available from:

Comress, 2 Research Court, Rockville, Maryland 20850
Comress (UK) Ltd., Alliance House, 29/30 High Holburn, London W.C.1,
    England

FORTUNE

This is a FORTRAN IV tuner that analyzes the source code and then executes the program, producing a report on the number of times each statement was executed, and at what cost. Price: $2490, or a one-time lease. Supplied by Computer Performance Systems, Inc., 3530 De La Cruz Blvd., Santa Clara, California 95050.

PROGRAM OPTIMIZATION

This is applicable to any third-generation COBOL. The system runs alongside an operational program, taking samples. The output is a report showing the amount of time spent in each paragraph and the number of times each paragraph was used. Price: $5000. Available from David R. Black, Computer Management Consultants, 1608 Investment Building, Pittsburgh, Pennsylvania 15222.

APPENDIX C | # KEY EVENTS IN THE EVOLUTION OF SOFTWARE

APPENDIX C.
Key Events in the
Evolution of Software

1801   Jacquard develops punch-card controlled loom.

1834   Babbage begins work on the Analytical Engine.

1887   Hollerith develops punch card equipment for 1890 U.S. Bureau of the Census.

1908   Powers invents the buffered keypunch.

1936   Turing publishes the concept of the "Universal Machine."

1944   Harvard Mark I goes into operation.
Von Neumann joins the ENIAC group at the University of Pennsylvania.

1945   The mercury storage tank makes computer-stored programs practical.
Von Neumann publishes his proposal for a stored-program computer.

1946   February 15: The ENIAC is dedicated.

1948   IBM introduces the Card Programmed Calculator (CPC) and the 604.
The transistor is invented.

1949   First operation of a stored program, on the EDSAC at Cambridge, England.

1950   First operation of a stored program in the United States, on the SEAC.

1951   The first commercial stored program computer, UNIVAC I, delivered to the U.S. Bureau of the Census.

1952   IBM 701 announced: First large-scale binary computer with programmable index registers.

1953   Magnetic core memory announced but it is still in the laboratory.
IBM 650 announced.

1954   Philco Corporation develops the surface-barrier transistor, making transistors practical for use in computers.
IBM begins development of FORTRAN.

1957   First practical use of FORTRAN on the 704.

1958   The ACM and GAMM meet in Zurich; ALGOL 58 published.
1959   First transistorized computers delivered; second generation begins.
        Development of COBOL begins.
1960   First use of a commercial programming language, FLOW-MATIC.
        The "Paris 13" meet; ALGOL 60 published.
1963   The "Three plus Three" committee formed to develop PL/1 specs.
1964   April 7: IBM announces System/360 and emulation: The third gen-
            eration begins.
1965   IBM announces the large-scale time-sharing System 360/67.
1966   April 1: The first PL/1 compiler is delivered.
1969   June: IBM unbundles in the United States.
        October: Codasyl Data Base Task Force publishes recommendations
            for DDL and DML.

REFERENCES

REFERENCES

1. J. Bairstow, "Proprietary Software Is Beginning to Grow Up." *Computer Decisions* (February 1971), pp. 30–31.
2. R. W. Bemer, "A Politico-Social History of Algol." In M. I. Halpern and C. J. Shaw (eds.) *Annual Review in Automatic Programming*, Vol. 5, pp. 151–237. New York: Pergamon Press, 1969.
3. R. P. Bigelow, "Legal Aspects of Proprietary Software." *Datamation* (October 1968), pp. 32–39.
4. R. P. Bigelow, "Contract Caveats." *Datamation* (Sept. 15, 1970), pp. 41–44.
5. M. Blee, "The Package Deal." *Data Systems* (November 1969), pp. 36–37.
6. J. Bonner, "Using System Monitor Output to Improve Performance." *IBM Systems Journal*, Vol. 8, No. 4 (1969), pp. 290–298.
7. "British Computer Software Protection." In *Report of Proceedings of the Legal Protection of Computer Programs of a Two-Day Conference*, November 1969.
8. H. Bromberg, "Software Buying," *Datamation* (Sept. 15, 1970), pp. 35–40.
9. P. J. Brown, "Using a Macro Processor to Aid Software Implementation." *The Computer Journal* (November 1969), pp. 327–331.
10. F. J. Buckley, "Verification of Software Programs." *Computers and Automation* (February 1971), pp. 23–24, 27.
10a. A. W. Burks, H. H. Goldstine, and J. Von Neumann, "Preliminary Discussion of the Logical Design of an Electronic Computing Instrument." Princeton, New Jersey: Institute for Advanced Study, 1946. Reprinted in *Datamation*, September 1962.
11. R. G. Canning, "Progress in Information Retrieval." *EDP Analyzer* (January 1970).
12. R. G. Canning, "Selecting New Products and Services." *EDP Analyzer* (July 1970).

13. R. G. Canning, "Trends in Data Management, Part I." *EDP Analyzer* (May 1971).

14. R. G. Canning, "Trends in Data Management, Part II." *EDP Analyzer* (June 1971).

15. R. G. Canning, "Application Packages Revisited." *EDP Analyzer* (July 1971).

16. H. N. Cantrell and A. L. Ellison, "Multiprogramming System Performance Measurement and Analysis." *AFIPS Conference Proceedings*, Vol. 32 (1968), SJCC, pp. 213-221.

17. J. W. Carr, "Programming and Coding." In F. M. Grabbe (ed.) *Handbook of Automation, Computation and Control.* New York: Wiley, 1959.

18. N. Chapin, "Perspective on Flowcharting Packages." *Computers and Automation* (March 1971), pp. 16-19, 26.

19. M. E. Conway, "On the Economics of the Software Market." *Datamation* (October 1968), pp. 28-31.

20. J. Cook, "Marketing a Package." *Data Systems* (April 1971), pp. 38-42.

21. G. Curtis and K. Falor, "Solve Your Software Headaches with a Generalized Program." *Computer Decisions* (February 1971), pp. 34-35.

22. E. F. Davis and J. L. Blose, "Tax Treatment of Software Costs." *Business Automation* (Feb. 1, 1971), pp. 42-45.

23. M. E. Drummond, Jr., "A Perspective on System Performance Evaluation." *IBM Systems Journal*, Vol. 8, No. 4 (1969).

24. J. P. Eckert, Jr., "In the Beginning and to What End." In *Computers and Their Future—Speeches Given at The World Computer Pioneer Conference, Llandudno, July 1970.* Llandudno, Wales: Richard Williams and Partners.

25. F. J. S. Edwards, "The Development of High-Level Programming Languages." *Supplement to O & M Bulletin* (August 1969).

26. R. Fisher, "Picking a Package." *Data Systems* (January 1971), pp. 14-15.

27. N. Foy, "Towards a Lingua Franca for Computers." *New Scientist and Science Journal* (June 1971), pp. 680-681.

28. N. Foy, "Getting the Best Deal on Timesharing Software." *Computer Decisions* (February 1971), pp. 32-33.

29. A. G. Fraser, "Software for Commercial Data Processing." *The Computer Bulletin* (December 1967), pp. 246-247.

30. D. J. Gorman, "The Place of the Program Package." *Data Processing* (May-June 1969), pp. 285-286.

31. J. W. Granholm, "Parfit Payroll." *Datamation* (April 15, 1971), pp. 37-38.

32. R. V. Head, "Protecting Packaged Programs." *Journal of Systems Management* (October 1969), pp. 40-41.

33. R. V. Head and E. F. Linick, "Software Package Acquisition." *Datamation* (October 1968), pp. 22-27.
34. G. M. Hopper, "Computer Software." In *Computers and Their Future—Speeches Given at the World Computer Pioneer Conference, Llandudno, July, 1970.* Llandudno, Wales: Richard Williams and Partners.
35. P. Hunter, "The Software House and the User—Part 2: Selecting a Software House." *Data Systems* (October 1969), pp. 28-29.
36. J. Katzenelson, "Documentation and the Management of a Software Project—A Case Study." *Software—Practice and Experience* (April–June 1971), pp. 147-157.
37. R. H. Kay, "The Management and Organisation of Large Scale Software Development Projects." *AFIPS 1969 SJCC Proceedings*, pp. 425-433.
38. D. W. Kerry, "Choosing Computers for the Post Office." *Computer Bulletin* (October 1967), p. 12.
39. D. E. Knuth, "Von Neumann's First Computer Program." *Computing Surveys* (December 1970), pp. 247-260.
40. K. R. London, *Decision Tables—A Practical Approach.* Princeton, N. J.: Auerbach Publishers Inc., 1972.
41. D. D. McCracken, "Whither APL?" *Datamation* (Sept. 15, 1970), pp. 53-57.
42. B. McKay, "The Software House and the User—Part I: What Is a Software House?" *Data Systems* (October 1969), pp. 26-27.
43. J. Mills, "The ABC for Buying Packages." *Computer Management* (May 1971), pp. 29-40.
44. D. J. Minni, "Implementing the Very Large Applications Software Package." *Datamation* (December 1969), pp. 141-144.
45. D. F. Parkhill, *The Challenge of the Computer Utility.* Reading, Mass.: Addison-Wesley, 1966.
45a. W. Rodgers, *Think: A Biography of the Watsons and IBM.* London: Weidenfeld and Nicholson, 1960.
46. S. Rosen, "Programming Systems and Languages: A History." *AFIPS Conference Proceedings*, Vol. 25, 1964, *SJCC*, pp. 1-15.
47. S. Rosen, "Electronic Computers: A Historical Survey." *Computing Surveys* (March 1969), pp. 7-36.
48. R. F. Rosin, "Supervisory and Monitor Systems." *Computing Surveys* (March 1969), pp. 37-54.
49. P. A. Samet, "Measuring the Efficiency of Software." *The Computer Bulletin* (October 1969), pp. 351-352.
50. P. A. Samet, "An Effective Assessment of Software." *Data Processing* (Jan.-Feb. 1970), pp. 45-47.

51. J. E. Sammet, "A Detailed Description of COBOL." In R. Goodman (ed.),
    Annual Review in Automatic Programming, Vol. 2. New York:
    Pergamon Press, 1961, pp. 197–230.
52. Steve Shirley, "Evaluating Benchmark Tests." *Data Systems* (September
    1969), pp. 31–33.
53. W. I. Stanley, "Measurement of System Operational Statistics." *IBM Sys-
    tems Journal*, Vol. 8, No. 4 (1969), pp. 299–308.
54. A. Taylor, "The FLOW-MATIC and MATH-MATIC Automatic Program-
    ming Systems." In R. Goodman (ed.), *Annual Review in Automatic
    Programming*, Vol. 1. New York: Pergamon Press, 1960, pp. 196–206.
54a. Alan M. Turing. "On Computable Numbers, with an Application to the
    Entscheidungs-problem [decisions/problems] ," *Proc.* London Math.
    Soc., Ser. 2-42, pp. 230–265.
55. H. Voysey, "Perspective in Recent Software Developments." *Software
    World* (Autumn 1969), p. 12.
56. L. Welke (ed.), "How to Buy Proprietary Software." Indianapolis, Ind.:
    International Computer Programs, Inc., 1970.
57. L. Welke, *ICP Software Newsletter* (September 1971).
58. T. A. Wise, "IBM's $5,000,000,000 Gamble." *Fortune*, Part I (September
    1966), p. 123ff; Part II (October 1966), p. 138ff.
59. W. J. Wittreich, "How to Buy/Sell Professional Services." *Harvard Business
    Review* (March–April 1966), pp. 127–138.

INDEX

INDEX